Motel W

D1096225

1st American ed 10th

Their Finest Hour

Their Finest Hour

*First-Hand Narratives
of the War in England*

Edited by

ALLAN A. MICHIE

and

WALTER GRAEBNER

HARCOURT, BRACE AND COMPANY, NEW YORK

PRINTED IN THE UNITED STATES OF AMERICA
BY QUINN & BODEN COMPANY, INC., RAHWAY, N. J.

DEDICATION

"Let us therefore address ourselves to our duty, so bear ourselves that if the British Commonwealth and Empire lasts for a thousand years men will still say, 'This was their finest hour!'"

PRIME MINISTER WINSTON CHURCHILL
House of Commons, June 18, 1940

ACKNOWLEDGMENTS

The obligations of the editors are many. We wish to express our appreciation to the narrators of *Their Finest Hour* for patiently telling us their stories. Thanks are also due to the editors of *Life* magazine for allowing us to reprint the articles in book form; to Carl Olsson and Mary Welsh who took down many of the narratives; to the British Government for the kind facilities accorded us; to William Vandivert and Hans Wild, *Life* staff photographers, George Rodger and James Jarché for permission to reprint their pictures; to *Illustrated* and *Picture Post* magazines, and to the British Ministry of Information for allowing us the use of their pictures; and to Elizabeth Crockett and Dorothy Dennis for assistance in preparing the manuscript and illustrations.

ALLAN A. MICHIE
WALTER GRAEBNER

London
December 20, 1940

vi

PUBLISHER'S NOTE

For a newspicture magazine like *Life* to develop a new word method for reporting war may be a journalistic paradox but the fact is that these articles grew directly out of the editorial necessity of conveying to *Life's* readers some sense of the personal drama implicit in the Battles of Flanders, of France and of Britain.

The Battles of World War II have been different in one respect from the battles of all the wars of the past: men as individuals, not as masses formed into huge armed fighting forces, have been winning the victories or going down as heroes in defeat. The military conquest of France was not accomplished by hordes of infantry but by men in planes and men in tanks. The escape of the B.E.F. from Dunkirk would not have been possible but for the bravery of the comparatively few R.A.F. fighter pilots who covered the retreat from the air. In the naval actions to date the massed battle fleets have remained in the background, leaving the enemy to the single ships and the small squadrons. Till the end of time man will marvel not at the armies entrenched for the defense of London but at the incredible fighting qualities of a few thousand young pilots who beat back wave after wave of Luftwaffe bombers.

Life's correspondents in London were instructed to "get the stories" of individuals who, in the mass, were making the thundering headlines of last May and June. These able journalists, with the permission of the British Ministry of Information, proceeded to ferret out a B.E.F. sergeant just back from Dunkirk, a R.A.F. squadron leader who helped make that great retreat possible, a flight sergeant who bombed the Ruhr, two seamen who survived the torpedoing of an armed merchant cruiser, a volunteer fireman who fought German incendiaries on the London docks. From each of these and others like them *Life's* correspondents skillfully extracted a first-person account of their experiences which *Life* was proud to print, and which the present publishers believe to be about the best contemporary literature on the war. These brief narratives are as simple and as direct and as devoid of literary flourishes as the men who tell them. That *Life's* correspondents could also be faithful to the formula they had invented and perfected for dealing with other peoples' stories when their turn came to tell their own story of being bombed, readers can see for themselves in "Cable 1301."

If these stories have a larger human value than their exciting narrative interest, it lies in their record of real bravery and true modesty that always go hand in hand.

CONTENTS

LIST OF ILLUSTRATIONS

xii

xiii

xiv

Twenty-One Days

by

SERGEANT JACK WADSWORTH

TWENTY-ONE DAYS

SERGEANT JACK WADSWORTH

TWENTY-ONE DAYS

MEN WAITING AT DUNKIRK

THE BEACH AT DUNKIRK: MEN

TWENTY-ONE DAYS

THE BEACH AT DUNKIRK: BOATS

I FOUGHT IN THE SKY OVER DUNKIRK

SPITFIRES IN FORMATION

I FOUGHT IN THE SKY OVER DUNKIRK

LAST CHECKUP

FIGHT TO THE FINISH

SIGNALMAN RONALD GOLD   CHIEF PETTY OFFICER FREDERICK G. BISHO

I BOMBED THE RUHR

ROYAL AIR FORCE PILOTS

BOMBER RETURNING FROM NIGHT FLIGHT OVER GERMANY

I BOMBED THE RUHR

ALL SET

I. TWENTY-ONE DAYS

A Story of the Great Retreat

ON THE black Tuesday of June 4, 1940, the last little British boat pulled out from Dunkirk and the last escaping member of the B.E.F. looked back on the curtain of smoke and flame that had fallen on the last act of the Battle of Flanders. Behind the curtain, lost to the Germans, were some thirty thousand British troops, one thousand guns, incalculable amounts of machine guns, trucks, tanks, armored cars, ammunition, food, and stores. Yet the retreat from Dunkirk, after all hope seemed lost, will live in the annals of the democracies as a great victory. The Germans had boasted that they would capture the British Army to a man. Once again, however, the British soldier proved that free men are always the world's most terrible fighters.

This is the story of one soldier who took part in the retreat. He is twenty-one-year-old Sergeant Jack Wadsworth, member of a Territorial battalion of a famous Midlands regiment. A Yorkshireman, he was studying to be a surveyor when war broke out. Sergeant Wadsworth led his platoon as part of the rear guard of the Flanders retreat, and was among the last evacuated from Dunkirk.

This is Wadsworth's story: There weren't any English newspapers in the far-off corner of western France where we had been putting in the final fortnight of our war training, so we weren't exactly in touch with events. But somebody in the camp had a radio that worked occasionally. It was that which told us on a Sunday that the Germans had invaded Holland and Belgium.

We knew what that meant and were glad. "Won't be long now," said the chaps. "Now for a smack at Jerry at last." We were trained to a hair and just fed up with waiting.

It was a lovely day, that last day in camp, real hot summer weather. There were no parades that afternoon, so I went out with another platoon sergeant, a pal of mine, who got it badly at Mount Cassel afterward. We strolled down through the French lanes watching the farm people at work, and down to the estaminet in the village. There we had several beers to ease the dust. We talked shop about our platoons, comparing notes about this man and that, and about what was likely to happen—the usual sort of army stuff. Dick said, "God, I'm glad to be here," and we had another.

Back at the camp there were rumors of an impending move, but that night we turned in as usual, as if the war had been a thousand miles away. The next morning, however, instead

4

of reveille at 6:30 A.M., we got a "fall-in" at 5:45. Men tumbled out just anyhow, but we didn't look so bad, especially my platoon. We were wide enough awake when the company commander came along.

He hadn't much to say—just "We're moving, men. I don't know when, and I don't know where. When you fall out you'll get your breakfasts. Then get everything ready." He waited a bit and then said he wondered if there was a man in the company who didn't feel as glad as he did now that the job was on for which we had come. We all roared out "No!" He gave a little grin at that and turned away.

The orders came that afternoon, and the battalion got on the little local train, which carried us down to the main-line station at Rennes. There was a long wait there under an avenue of trees while all the battalion supplies were put on board. A battalion is not an easy thing to move. It can't be done in an hour. But at 10:30 that night we entrained and, dog-tired by now, got down to sleep.

All that night, the next day, and another night and day the train rumbled on—if rumbling is the word, because there were constant long stops. Sometimes we pulled into sidings while faster trains filled with supplies went past. On the second day we saw trainloads of refugees go by in the opposite direction. We went by circuitous routes. We had plenty to eat, though it was mostly canned stuff. I found out then

5

that a clasp knife with a good can-opener at the end is just about the soldier's best friend.

At some stops the cooks dashed across the platforms with their dixies and tea and sugar all ready for the boiling water, which must have been wired for ahead. I've heard that troops going up the line in the last war had to scrounge water from the engine for their tea. In this war we got this tea-water problem better organized. The washing problem hasn't been solved, though. When we got to the end of the journey we were as black as sweeps.

The end came at a place called Seclin, south of Lille. We lined up outside the station, and no sooner were we in some sort of order than there was an air-raid warning. It was the first time most of us had heard one, and you should have seen the rush, including the officers, to get the Brens fixed on their anti-aircraft mountings. But all our eagerness was wasted. We caught just one glimpse of three Jerry aircraft very high up. A couple of our fighters came across toward them and they cleared off.

After a clean-up and some food in an orchard, we crossed a bridge over the railway track, and there we saw a reason for our stopping so short of the Belgian frontier. Up the line toward the east there was the wreckage of a great German bomber right across the rails, which were twisted apart. Breakdown gangs were at work. On the other side of the bridge we embussed into great lorries and set off again, still not knowing exactly where we were going.

It was near the Belgian frontier that we ran into our first real glimpse of the war. Our lorries dropped from 30 m.p.h. to a snail's pace, because of the stream of refugees pouring toward France and packing the roads with every kind of vehicle that could move and some that couldn't. It was the sight of these people—the old men and women, the tired, frightened children—that made the boys mad. It put fresh heart into them to get at Jerry, tired though we all were from nearly four days with no rest except cat naps in the jolting train.

At last we came to the place which turned out to be our assigned position—a place called Oomburgen, about forty miles west of Brussels and astride a main road from the capital.

We debussed there shortly before dusk into more orchards, and then saw something of the German Air Force. They were coming over, medium dive bombers at no great height, in droves of thirty at a time. What beats me is why they didn't plaster the main road, which by this time was packed with traffic, military and refugee, going all ways, but mostly west.

Watching that traffic, it dawned on me then—and on most of us—that instead of taking part in an advance, we were really taking part in a retreat. All we had done was to get far enough up to become a rear guard. You must remember that we had had no news for days of what had been happening. That day would have been, I think, the fifteenth. One of our chaps who could speak French had learned from some refugees that there was heavy fighting going on around Brussels.

That night we slept in barns round Oomburgen. The cookers had got up, and we had the first good hot meal since we started. There were stringent blackout orders, and it was just my luck as orderly sergeant to be up most of the night, stumbling round in the darkness to see that the orders were carried out. All through the night I could hear the Jerry aircraft droning about far above in great numbers. Their sound reminded me of the wild geese we'd hear on winter nights crossing the Yorkshire moors.

In the morning we learned what our job was. The whole battalion was to line up at intervals along this main road to keep traffic going, keep refugees off the roads and in the fields, and adopt such action against advancing enemy as became necessary.

We got our anti-tank guns in position by 5 A.M. The refugees were a big problem. Speaking mostly Flemish, they could not understand us, nor we them. If they were ordered off the roads by gestures, they pretended not to understand, and dully plodded along, or else started wailing and just sat down. You can't push women and kids about, and we scarcely knew what to do till one of us hit on the idea of seizing the leaders, pointing skyward, and then to the road and saying with horrible grimaces: "Une bombe." Then we'd point to the fields, smile, and wave cheerily. That worked all right.

As we were getting the road clear, the rumble of gunfire in the distance was growing nearer. Early that morning we let a Guards battalion through—or what was left of them. They had been in some heavy fighting, we were told, trying to stem the German advance across the Albert Canal. But they were cheerful and swinging along as if they were moving up Buckingham Palace Road.

At midday, having had no actual contact yet with the Germans, we also were ordered to withdraw. The traffic down the road was now a mere trickle. It was disheartening, but we were told that there were not enough of us to do any good, and, besides, our position was "in the air." We marched —the first of a lot of marching—till 1:30 A.M. We had covered about twenty-five miles when some of the battalion got rest in an old abandoned farmhouse. I slept in a hencoop, on the floor under the perches—and was glad of it.

The next day we covered another twenty miles and found an empty village to rest in. As soon as it was light, the Germans began bombing and machine-gunning the village. Though the raid went on for a couple of hours and the village street was packed with our transport, there were no casualties. Anti-aircraft fire spoiled their aim and drove them off. Throughout all the days afterward I never saw Jerry aircraft press home an attack against any opposition. They don't like reasonably accurate fire, and I've seen the appearance of a single Spitfire clear the sky like magic of half a dozen German bombers.

Again it was marching—twenty miles the next day and twenty the next, always with the German bombers coming over in droves, bombing and machine-gunning. We kept together and pressed doggedly on. Now and then we'd see a great pillar of smoke in front or behind as bombs landed, and we'd hear the shout "Stretcher bearers!" passed along the line. On the whole we had few casualties. By now we were good at getting to cover off the road as soon as the raiders approached.

That second day we were beginning to tire badly under the long forced marches in full kit and the continual bombing, but in the afternoon we passed the Guards battalion which had passed through our lines on the Brussels road three days before. They were eating by the roadside, and they must have done seventy-five miles in those three days. They gave us a bit of a cheer as we went past, and I'm afraid that we, knowing that we were the youngest battalion in the British Army, showed off a bit in front of those Guards, pulling ourselves together and practically marching at attention.

That night we got to Seclin—back to where we had started five days before. There transport picked us up and rushed us through the night to a point seven miles from Douai. We could see the city burning on the skyline. Some of the men fell asleep where they stood as we waited in the darkness for orders. There was a continuous roar of artillery fire and bombing toward Douai, and the sky was ablaze with "contact" lights sent up by the Germans. At last orders came. We were told to dig in along the canal bank nearby. The opposition was about five miles away toward Douai, and we were to hold them.

We got well down by dawn, and then for two days got a taste of the real thing in the way of bombing. They bombed us to hell. Every few minutes from dawn till dark the dive bombers came over in relays. They'd come in flocks overhead and then form a line. The leader would turn over and come down. You'd hear the high, screaming crescendo of his motor and then the sound of the bomb that seemed to be coming right at you. The terrific "whump" of the explosion made you gasp and seemed to split your skull. Soon we learned to distinguish between bombs. A whistling sound meant that it was some distance away. A sheet-ripping sound meant nearby.

Personally, I didn't do much thinking about anything, but it did me good to keep my thoughts on my platoon and go along the section posts. If you have got the wind up, having something to do helps. I had the wind up a lot, especially during the first day of concentrated bombing along that canal-bank trench line. I had the real taste of it in my mouth. Somehow it tasted like a penny I once popped in my mouth when I was a kid. But when you are an N.C.O. you mustn't show it.

Once, crouching under a huge salvo of bombs that sent showers of trench parapet down on top of me, a phrase of the Commander in Chief flashed through my mind. He had said that war was days of intense boredom mixed with moments of acute fear. I suddenly realized how true it was and burst out laughing, until I saw the next man along looking at me queerly.

After two days in this position, with no Germans yet in sight, we were moved farther to the right and told to dig in again by the canal bank, covering two bridges that were ruined. Jerry was a mile away, hidden behind a knoll over which he lobbed mortar fire. He came no nearer, but the same bombing went on and now shells began to arrive. Still we had comparatively few casualties—because of the way we looked after ourselves, I suppose.

After three days there, we were hurriedly moved out as the enemy were past our flanks. We marched from 10:30 at night till 4:30 in the morning, when our transport picked us up dead-beat and brought us into Armentières. The town was being heavily bombed, but they didn't stay long when our fighters turned up. Our convoy went through. Unfortunately, nearly half of it was misdirected and went on toward Mount Cassel instead of toward Steenvorde. Going down the valley, they ran bang under Jerry's guns placed along a bridge. They got hell and lost a lot of men. I only heard that afterward, when the remnants rejoined us for the last stand in front of Dunkirk.

My convoy of about half the battalion went on toward Steenvorde. Near there we went through the most intensive bombing we had yet experienced. The afternoon sky seemed black with dive bombers. Before we could get to field cover, a salvo hit some of the lorries in front, killing or wounding every man inside. A company sergeant major who had got it badly in the side and arm was lying in the road when I got up, shouting, "Leave me, leave me!" Some of his company carried him off the road through the machine-gun spray and the bomb blasts, and they were getting a dressing on him in a field bomb hole within a minute or two.

We just stuck it there till night came and the bombers cleared out. Then we went into the village. No sooner were we settled down than I was sent for and detailed to take a section out to a forked road at midnight and set up anti-tank guns covering one of the forks. The company dug in in the darkness, and my officer told me that we were now covering a main line of retreat for other troops through to Dunkirk. Their road lay off somewhere to our left. We had to stop anything coming in from the right to cut them off.

We lay there till dawn. Though Jerry was shelling heavily, I nearly fell asleep at the guns once or twice. What kept jerking me back each time I drowsed was a little stray dog we had picked up. He was cuddled under my arm and kept on shoving his cold nose against my wrist. It was a funny thing about those dogs. Scores of them followed us through the retreat. We used to think it was because they knew we were English. At night they slept with us in barns, huddled up against the men they had picked out. There was one we called our "air-raid warning," a little black-and-white mongrel. He could spot the difference between dive bombers and any other. When we were in a village he would come pelting into the billet as they came over and bury his nose and shiver against the man he had been following.

Before that dawn broke we got another set of orders. We were told that our battalion had been selected to make a last stand along the right flank of what they now call the Corunna Line and to hold the last gate open for the troops to get through to Dunkirk. We knew it was an honor for the work we had already done because we were to hold this last line with some remnants of the Guards and a picked battalion of the French Army. There were also some of the Green How-ards, who, on the left of us at Douai, had smashed up a Ger-man mass attack and then, like the Camerons, had gone in with the bayonet. They had killed thousands. I had watched the Germans coming over on our left at that place, and they struck me then like chaps who were being driven on from behind. They went into machine-gun fire all night, though they were being mowed down. That struck me as being plain silly in men who are supposed to be soldiers. But they couldn't stand cold steel. That's what broke them—when the Green Howards and the Camerons smashed up nearly a division. We were longing for the same chance.

We went back two miles and were now six miles from Dun-kirk. There we dug in on the banks of the Bergues Canal, facing west and south. Water from the smashed locks was helping to form another barrier on our right. On our left were the roads, the gateway through which thousands of troops were pouring to the beaches. Our neighbors, the French, were also digging in. I thought they were marvelous chaps. Our artillery, battery after battery, was forming in the pocket between us, having passed through the gap we had kept open.

We had just got chin-down in the trenches when it started. First came endless relays of dive bombers, then the shelling from the guns we had brought up behind the retreating army.

Those two days were the worst, and we had heavy casualties. The second day Jerry got up to the woods in front of the trenches, but we kept up such a barrage of machine-gun fire in the woods that nothing came out of them. Over our heads, our guns behind were keeping up drumfire into the enemy positions. Attack after attack was smashed and we must have lost a lot. It was an inferno, but I think our stuff was heavier than theirs.

At night the stream of troops through the gap died down and we were ordered to retire on Dunkirk. But the Germans had the road ranged, and we turned off three miles to rest. It took us twelve hours to cover the six miles into Dunkirk.

We found Dunkirk a mass of ruins, with fires everywhere and thousands waiting on the beaches. On the right was a mile-long jetty, badly bomb-torn. We queued up and walked along it in our thousands in the darkness. I did think that it wouldn't be nice to be caught here when daylight and the bombers arrived. So did lots of others, I suppose, but everything was orderly and quiet as we moved along, the less-tired ones holding the others up.

When my batch got to the end, we found two destroyers there. The way the Navy got us on board in that pitch darkness, lit only by shellfire, was a miracle of speed and coolness. The whole destroyer seemed to be loaded in less than half an hour. We slid out to sea, leaning over with the weight of men aboard. Daylight was just breaking when we cleared the harbor. Along the coast I could see the glare of fires in villages and towns all the way down to Calais. The skies inland were ablaze with Very lights and bursting shrapnel. That was the last thing I saw or heard before we got to England, because I fell asleep. I did hear alarm bells and a shout of "Man action stations forward," but I didn't care.

Looking back through all those twenty-one days, the queer thing is that not once did my company have a real go at Jerry. That's all I want now. In a few days we'll be O.K. and ready again. . . .

I Fought in the Sky over Dunkirk

by an

R.A.F. SQUADRON LEADER

II. I FOUGHT IN THE SKY OVER DUNKIRK

THE success of the Dunkirk evacuation was due in great part to the British fighter planes, which, against terrific odds, kept command of the air over Dunkirk and the Channel.

The author of this chapter, who must adhere to the R.A.F. tradition of anonymity, is a tall, quiet-mannered, twenty-five-year-old squadron leader. He is a Londoner. Four years ago, before the outbreak of war, he passed his final examinations as an electrical engineer at Liverpool University, and after some flying with the University Auxiliary Squadron, he took a short service commission in the R.A.F. because he liked flying and wanted to see some fun before settling down to a job. Like most fighter pilots, he doesn't worry too much about the future. "I just want to keep on troubling the Huns a bit more," he says.

During the Dunkirk show he flew an unarmed two-seater trainer from a base in the south of England, landed on the bomb-holed Calais Marck airport, and picked up a wounded squadron leader under the noses of an attacking force of twenty Messerschmitts. For this feat, he was awarded the D.S.O.

This is his story: We got a "stand by" early in the morning of the first day of the Dunkirk evacuation, and at 9 A.M. we got our orders. There were twelve of us and, climbing to 20,000 feet, we headed across the North Sea. I don't remember many personal impressions of that first journey out, except the feeling that here was something really doing at last. You must remember that for many weeks we had carried out offensive patrols up to the French and Belgian coastline, but had never seen any Huns. I remember being slightly worried about my engine, but somehow in a single-engine one always has slight quirks of mind about the motor when one is flying over the sea; perhaps it is the difference in the sound that does it.

We kept well together, but of course kept radio silence. We knew every inch of the coastline to which we were heading, but even without that knowledge there was no mistaking it was Dunkirk. Only a few minutes after leaving Britain, and at our height, we could see the pillars of smoke arising from the burning town and the villages all the way up from Calais. The horizon was one vast pall. We went right across the city and settled down to patrolling on a fifty-mile-long beat, but we saw nothing and decided to come downstairs.

At 4,000 feet we were beetling along still looking for trouble when I saw a Hun formation of about sixty machines—twenty bombers and forty fighters—at about 15,000 feet, and cursed the height we had lost. The fighters, mostly Messerschmitts, heeled over and came screaming down at us, and the next second we were in the thick of it. That attack developed, like most dogfights, into individual scraps. It was at about 10,000 feet that I found myself on the tail of my first Hun, a Messerschmitt 110. Most of my instruments, I remember, had gone haywire in the course of the violent maneuvering. I remember particularly that my giro was spinning crazily, and the artificial horizon had vanished somewhere into the interior of the instrument panel, calmly turning up its bottom and showing me the maker's stamp and the words "Air Ministry Mark IV," or something like that.

Down went the Messerschmitt again, with me close on his tail. With the great speed of the dive my controls were freezing solid, and I was fighting the stick hard to bring the Hun up into the center of my sights. When you get them there, they stick; in fact, it's hard to get them out. Once there you can hold them forever. I thumbed the trigger button just once, twice. I smelt the cordite fumes blowing back from my Brownings as the 1,200 squirts a minute from each of them went into him. I saw the little spurts of flame as the tracers struck. For a fraction of a second I saw the back outline of the pilot's head half slewed around to see what was after him, presumably before he ceased to know. I saw a burst of flame and smoke from his engine, and then he was going down in a twirling spin of black smoke.

I looked around for the rest, but they were gone. My own scrap had brought me about thirty miles inland, so I turned and headed back, noticing with a shock that my petrol reserve was just enough to get me home, provided that I ran into no more trouble. Dogfighting uses up juice at an enormous rate. About that first fight—when you're going into it you think "What fun," and when it's over you think "How bloody dangerous." Out over the North Sea and on the way back to the station I clicked on the radio and called up the pilots of my squadron one by one: "How are you? Did you get any?" The first one came back jubilantly—he had got one. Then the rest—all of them had got one or two. One was funny. When I asked him what he had got, he came back, growling and disgusted, with "a Graf Zeppelin." Two didn't answer.

Back at the station we refueled, reloaded, and were off again in a quarter of an hour. Back over Dunkirk at 10,000 feet we ran into a whole flock of Messerschmitts which came charging down out of the clouds. They had obviously been

24

sitting upstairs guarding some bombers hidden in the smoke below. They nearly caught us. I saw tracers going past my ears, and actually heard the gun rattle from one on my tail, and then he was gone. I followed him down, banging the throttle open and leaning on my stick, but in the last smoke clouds hanging over Dunkirk I lost him.

Up again, I saw the rest of the squadron at about 6,000. They were in a hell of a mix-up with Hun fighters and some Junkers 88's, and I climbed up to join them. My radio was open, and as I climbed I could hear a stream of occasionally comic backchat passing backward and forward between some of the other members of the squadron, occasionally punctuated with bursts of gunfire as they were popping off at Huns. Once, for instance, I heard a New Zealander calling and saying calmly, "There's a Messerschmitt on your tail," and the reply, "O.K., pal," and then I was in it too.

I picked out a Junkers 88 whose tail gunner got onto me as soon as I engaged. The tracers of his guns sheered past me, seeming to curve lazily past my clear-vision window. You watch them quite calmly. They never look as though they were going to hit you, even when they are practically dead on. Again there was that lovely feeling of the gluey controls and the target being slowly hauled into the sights. Then thumb down on the trigger again and the smooth shuddering of the machine as the eight-gun blast let go. This time the squirt I gave him must have cut him in two. His tail folded back on his wings and there was a great smoke and flash of flame as he went down. As I spiraled down slowly after him, keeping a lookout for more, I saw one man bail out and his chute open.

The sky was nearly clear of Huns, and I turned round for home again, calling up the squadron as I went. This time we were all there, but our total bag was better than the first show. We had got eleven in all, making nineteen in one morning for our two.

The second day we had a defined objective, but I detached two pilots to do some free-lance patrolling, one above the clouds, which were at about 12,000 feet over Dunkirk, and the other about 2,000 below. The rest of us went off toward Calais. About halfway there I heard the one above the clouds calling to the other in a deliberately affected sort of actor's voice, "Oh, look what's coming, dearie, hordes and hordes of Messerschmitts. Nasty Messerschmitts." And the answer back, "O.K., pal, keep them busy. I'm coming upstairs."

We swung round and started back. Making the quick turn out to sea, I saw some Junkers guarded by Messerschmitts bombing a torpedo boat and some small rescue craft packed with troops far below. Chancing the anti-aircraft fire from the torpedo boat, we plunged in. The Huns never saw us coming. Every one of us got one in that first dive. Stick back and screaming up again, we re-formed, and then down once more. This time the Huns had scattered and it wasn't so easy. I got onto one Messerschmitt who was scramming for home and got a squirt in. There was the usual burst of smoke from his engine as he went down. I followed, and I'm glad I did. Biding my time, I let him have it.

I didn't know then how they had got on with the Messerschmitt swarm they had run into above Dunkirk, but on the way back the first to answer my radio call said that he had got four. Then he suddenly said, "Oh, hell, my engine's packed up." Then, "I'm on fire." There was silence for a second or two, and he said, "Yippee! There's a destroyer downstairs. I'm bailing out." A second later I heard him mutter, "But how?"

It is, as a matter of fact, not easy to bail out of a Spitfire. The best way is to turn her over on her back and drop out through the hood—if you can. That, we found out later, was exactly what he had done. He turned up in the mess three days afterward wearing a naval sublieutenant's jacket and bell-bottom trousers, and carrying a sailor's kitbag over his shoulder.

That day, for all its excitement, was a poorer bag than we had expected—a total of eleven. The third day we had the biggest show of all, because then the evacuation was in full swing and the Hun was throwing in everything he had in the way of aircraft to smash up the proceedings. We were now starting off at dawn, and on that day we went over Dunkirk and back again twice before breakfast time, and my squadron was in thirty different combats.

On the second occasion my squadron ran into the biggest cloud of fighters that I'd seen so far. They were all Messerschmitt 109's, and there must have been pretty nearly one hundred of them. They seemed like a swarm of bees. We went in, however, and tore off a chunk each. My recollections of that show are a bit hazy, because we were fighting upstairs and downstairs between 1,000 and 15,000 feet, and I was blacking-out fairly often in the pull-outs after diving after a Hun. But I'm certain I got four, and the rest of the squadron wasn't doing too badly, because at one time the air seemed to be full of burning aircraft. They were enemy planes all right, because we lost only one machine in that mad half-hour. The pilot of that one had his ailerons blown away but managed to land on Dunkirk beach. He had a big gash in his forehead but managed to radio operations room at our station that he had "landed safely." He got onto Dunkirk jetty that night and came home with some of the B.E.F., getting back in mess that afternoon.

After finishing this first scrap with the 109's, we ran into another bunch of 110's. We certainly got three Messerschmitts. They can dive very fast indeed. On that afternoon I remember following a Messerschmitt down from 15,000 and my needle had gone twice round the clock and off altogether before I decided to pull out. I must have been doing nearly

550 m.p.h. when I pulled out, but the Hun was still going. I think he went altogether into the ditch. All I remember is that I could not get the stick back but had to use the tail-adjusting gear to pull out.

Instantly I felt the familiar blackout symptoms come on again, first the light turning yellow, then red, then slow darkness. You seem to be conscious, but you can't see nor, I think, hear, because when you come out there is a sudden roar, much louder than the ordinary sound of the motor.

That blooding we got over Dunkirk was instructive to all of us. Personally, I don't think that most of the Hun pilots are very good. I have come across a few who seem to enjoy fighting, but the bulk of them don't. They simply don't know their stuff. And our aircraft are certainly better.

They have got the numbers all right—or had—but I am more than ever sure that, however outnumbered you may be in dogfights at high speed, it boils down at any given moment to man against man.

Since this chapter was written, the death of one of the pilots who took part in the action makes it possible to reveal his name. He was twenty-three-year-old Acting Pilot Officer John Laurence Allen, D.F.C. The narrator of the story was his squadron leader.

Allen's career with the R.A.F. had brought him into the news before. On the morning of January 18, 1938, while

flying a training machine, he disappeared in the fog over For-
farshire, Scotland. Search parties failed to find him that afternoon or night. Early next morning an R.A.F. search plane
spotted a wrecked machine on snow-covered Glen Dye moor
in Kincardineshire. Beside the plane lay twelve men of a rescue party, spelling out the word A-L-I-V-E. An ambulance
plane was rushed to the spot. Young Allen, although badly
injured, had refused to abandon his machine until rescuers
arrived.

It was on May 31, 1940, while the battle of Dunkirk was
on, that his squadron leader flew an unarmed trainer to the
Calais Marck airport. Allen and several other pilots of the
squadron circled above the airport in their Spitfires, and when
twenty Messerschmitts swooped on the trainer they shot down
three, damaged three, and chased the others away. A few days
later, while flying alone between Calais and Dunkirk, he ran
into thirty Junkers 88's, promptly attacked them, and managed to damage one before the others high-tailed into the
clouds.

On June 28, for these and other exploits, Allen received
the D.F.C. from the King.

The forty-first Air Ministry casualty list, published a
month later, listed the name of Acting Pilot Officer John
Laurence Allen, D.F.C., as "killed in action while flying in
operations against the enemy."

Fight to the Finish

by

CHIEF PETTY OFFICER FREDERICK G. BISHOP

and

SIGNALMAN RONALD GOLD

III. FIGHT TO THE FINISH

HIGH in British Navy annals of World War II rank the exploits of two armed merchant cruisers, the *Rawalpindi*, which went down with colors flying after a running fight with the Nazi pocket battleship *Deutschland*, and the *Scotstoun*.

The 17,000-ton *Scotstoun*, before the war the Anchor Liner *Caledonia*, shuttled back and forth along Britain's North Atlantic Patrol until the morning of June 13, 1940. Armed with 6-inch guns mounted on her promenade decks, her holds packed with empty barrels and oil drums to give her extra buoyancy, she was under the command of white-haired, fatherly Captain S. K. ("Go Get 'Em") Smythe. The *Scotstoun's* crew of three hundred and fifty—two-thirds of them Royal Navy men and the rest Reservists from the Merchant Service—slept in the passenger cabins. Her dance-halls, restaurants, and lounges had been converted into magazines for cordite and shells, "sick bays" (hospitals on naval vessels), and operating theaters. Her record of prize and contraband seizures was higher than that of any other armed merchant cruiser.

On June 13, the *Scotstoun* was eighteen hours out of port after her periodical turn-round and revictualing. She was far to the northwest of the Hebrides and was rapidly approaching her assigned beat on the Northern Patrol. It was a sunless morning of dull, low clouds, with a moderate but exceptionally cold wind blowing off the melting ice floes. The ship was rolling heavily in the long Atlantic swells. At 6:15 A.M. the gun crews had been piped to practice action stations.

Suddenly, at 6:18, the *Scotstoun* was struck under the stern by a torpedo, which crippled her. At exactly 6:48 she was hit amidships by two more torpedoes that blew up a magazine. At 7:18 she sank. During that hour her gunners fought their hidden U-boat adversaries until their guns were submerged, when Captain Smythe gave orders to abandon ship.

By amazing good work and good luck, her whole complement, except two officers and four ratings, was saved. It was a miracle that any survived. The two U-boats which attacked had a "sitter" in the crippled liner and should have blown her out of the water. Only the courage, endurance, and marksmanship of her gun crews—and perhaps the timidity of the U-boat commanders—enabled the men to get safely away. The gunners, who passed shells high overhead as water swirled around their waists, believe they sent one U-boat to the bottom halfway through the fight.

Chief Petty Officer Bishop, who, as the doctor's first assistant, was stationed in the sick bay, saw the action taking place below decks. Born in Portsmouth, wiry forty-two-year-old Bishop, a pensioner after twenty-two years of service in the Navy when war broke out, was called up from his peacetime job as first-aid attendant in a London Kodak factory to join the *Scotstoun*.

Signalman Gold, twenty-five years old, went to the *Scotstoun* from the London Division of the Royal Naval Volunteer Reserve. In peacetime he worked in the advertising department of the Ingersoll Watch Company. Gold saw the *Scotstoun's* last fight from the bridge, where he rushed, clad only in shirt and pants, after the first torpedo struck.

CHIEF PETTY OFFICER BISHOP: I had heard the gun crews piped for practice and was already awake when the first torpedo struck. It was a stunning, sickening sensation, and the ship seemed to jolt to a standstill, just as if it had run up against a cushiony wall. The shock flung me out of my bunk, and while I was picking myself up, my ears still ringing with the explosion, the alarm buzzers started. I heard afterward that this first torpedo had shattered the steering gear and screws, rendering the ship helpless. It had also ripped open the

35

after hold, throwing most of the buoyancy cargo out onto the sea, and had wrecked the wireless aerial. The ship was settling by the stern.

I went at once to my action station in the sick bay, two decks below, saw the attendants assembled, and started laying out morphia, syringes, lint, and bandages, collecting surgical instruments, and stripping the operating tables, ready for the arrival of the doctor. Of course, I didn't know what had happened except that it was something serious, because after a colossal din the engines had stopped and we were rolling so heavily it was hard to keep one's feet. I remember thinking it would be a tough job for us all when the casualties started to come. But I kept busy on the routine jobs of preparation, because that helps to keep one's mind off guessing and wondering what is happening upstairs.

All the same, it was a relief when I heard the guns start thundering out and knew that, whatever it was, we were hitting back. The doctor came in just then and greeted us with a grin and a quick, approving nod at what we had done. He had been the *Scotstoun's* doctor in peacetime, by the way—a young Scotsman named Burns, and as cool a customer as I have ever known. It seemed that only about ten minutes had gone by (afterward I knew it was nearly half an hour, but it's amazing how quickly time passes when you are concentrated like we were), and I was having a last check over when

I noticed that the instrument dishes were not big enough for my liking. I remembered that I had a very big developing tray up in my cabin—I go in a bit for photography in my spare time—and, going across to the doctor and bawling above the noise of the gunfire, I asked permission to go up and get it. I reached my cabin and had just got my hands on the tray when the second explosion occurred. That was the two torpedoes blowing up the magazine near the sick bay at the end of the first half-hour.

It was the most terrific bang I have ever heard in my life, and it knocked me out for a moment. I came to lying on the floor in total darkness, because all the lights had gone out. The sudden list which the ship had taken had slid me up against some wall. But, strangely enough, I was still clutching the developer tray. Groping round, I found the door and got it open. Volumes of smoke and cordite fumes blew in. Still groping along in the blackness and leaning sideways against the list, I found my way along the alleyways down toward the sick bay. I thought, "What's the use, they must all be gone now, and the ship's going too." But, of course, your action station *is* your action station until relieved or ordered away. And the guns overhead were still thudding away.

There was one bad moment at the last companionway down. I put my foot out from the top step and there was nothing there! Luckily, I was holding the handrail. Pulling myself together, I went round another way and got into the dispensary, and there, like an absolute miracle, were the others with the doctor, who was holding a torchlight. Apparently they had followed the doctor into the dispensary to carry out some more materials when the explosion took place. The ambulatory (dressing center), where they had stood a few minutes before, was now a gaping hole right down to the interior of the ship. Everything had vanished—floor, tables, and all— and you could see the sky through the blown deck tiers above.

Following the doctor's torch, we made our way up to the main promenade deck and there learned that the order had been given to take to the boats. The ship was now leaning right over, with the edge of the main decks awash. With my sick bay party I went forward toward my boat station, but very slowly, in case there were wounded to be picked up and attended to among the wreckage. We passed gun crew after gun crew still at it and up to the waists in water. A lot were stripped down to pants and shirt in case they might soon have to swim for it, but they grinned at us as we passed. Looking out over the sea toward the great plumes from the fall of shot, I noticed that it was covered with floating barrels which had been blown out from the ship's insides. And as we passed the last gun crew, I actually heard them singing above the noise of the firing, "Roll out the Barrel," bawling the words out as they were passing the shells and ramming them home.

I got to my boat station and found the boat already nearly full and in the water. Sliding down the falls—a tricky business, because in the swell the boat was up one minute and down the next—I got in and we pushed away from the sinking ship. In the boat, I am not ashamed to say, I passed out for a bit. But a lot of us were pretty well done in, lying about across the thwarts. And some were sick because of the wild motion of the boat after the ship and the shock and strain of the past hour, and because of hunger. None of us had had food since supper the night before.

SIGNALMAN GOLD: I reported to the killick [Navy slang for leading signalman, so-called from the anchor or killick he wears as a sleeve badge] and got my orders to get as many ensigns up as I could. Getting up an ensign on each available mast is always a first step when a warship goes into action. The ensign goes up and stays up till the ship goes down. We get as many up as we can in case some are shot away. I managed to get three ensigns hoisted on the fore, main, and on the gaff aft. It wasn't easy, because the wireless aerial was in a tangle on the decks, and the after mast was leaning over all skewwhiff as a result of the first torpedo unseating it from its housing.

That job done, I decided to get back to my cabin for my trousers—the wind was pretty cold—before the list got so bad that I couldn't get there. Then I reported back to the bridge. From the bridge, in between my jobs, I had a good view of the action, and from the other signalman I learned a lot about the beginning of it. Nobody seems to have spotted the source of the attack before the first torpedo struck. Our attackers turned out to be two oceangoing U-boats far out on the starboard quarter, their periscopes barely feathering and hidden in the sea spume which overlay the heavy swell. But the alarm had sounded immediately on the klaxons, and a few minutes later the 6-inch and stern high-angle guns began their uproar. The ship lay wallowing in the trough of the swells, a wide-open target, and torpedo after torpedo came at her from the hidden submarines, which, however, were kept at a distance by the gun barrage.

The gun crews could see the torpedoes coming at them; they even caught sight of the colored ring markings on the warheads as they skimmed through the wave tops. Throughout the action one of the stern high-angle guns, depressed to its lowest point, was actually firing at the torpedoes and managed to divert several from their course. I myself saw at least six bounce out of the water and go speeding harmlessly past the ship.

I could see the marvelous high-angle gun on the stern hard at it pumping shot in front of the torpedo wakes, which kept coming at us. I distinctly saw one coming toward the beam and held my breath till it suddenly swerved and hurtled past, all glinting silver.

And I saw something else. Just as I got to the bridge I saw a radio operator coming down from the broken after mast. Somehow he had managed to climb up that mast and re-rig the aerial, and now he was racing toward the wireless cabin. I learned afterward that within three minutes of reaching the radio room, he had managed to get a code message over. Those three minutes helped to save us, because a minute later the two last torpedoes hit us, wrecking the wireless apparatus and the aerial—for good this time. The next minutes are a bit of a blank, with the ship listing slowly over the whole time. But I remember watching the water creeping up round the gun crews hard at work on the 6-inchers. First knee-deep, then waist-deep in water, they held the shells high above their heads as they fed the guns. Then, as the increasing angle of the sinking ship put one gun out of action, they moved on to another.

It's not my job to dish out praise, but I thought those men were great. All of them had seen the wrecked wireless aerial and knew that they had little hope of assistance or rescue (they didn't know, as I did, that, thanks to that radio operator's job of work, a three-minute message had got through). They were hundreds of miles away from the steamship lanes, and over a week's boat journey away from the nearest land.

British warships were unlikely to visit the area, and the relief vessel on this beat would not be due for a long time. But they kept on.

Finally, as gun after gun was submerged, the order came, "Abandon ship." I saw the captain come out of the control tower, stalk down the starboard wing of the bridge, and stare along the side. He was hatless, his white hair blowing about in the wind. We waited, but we weren't surprised when he half turned round and said over his shoulder, "Take to the boats." The message was passed on, and one after another the gun crews went to their boat stations or slid over the side onto rafts. But the stern high-angle gun kept on firing to the end, with two of its dead crew, killed during the first explosion, washing about in the waves at its base. But at length even that stopped, and the gunners climbed up the steeply sloping deck and joined the captain, the doctor, the chief gunnery instructor, and the rest of us on the bridge.

The killick came out with the confidential code books and handed some to me. It is his responsibility to see that these books go to the bottom as soon as the "abandon ship" order is given. Before I left the bridge to make my way down into a lifeboat, I heard the captain say to the other officers, "Well, I don't think we have done so badly, gentlemen. We've still got three ensigns up and the guns going." When I had slid down into the boat I looked up and saw the captain holding grimly on to the bridge rail. I could see that he was ordering the other officers over the side. But for their answer, at a nod from the first lieutenant, the little group seized him by the arms and plunged with him down the sloping bridge and into the water, where another boat picked them up.

Some of the men were singing as we pulled away to watch the *Scotstoun* go down. It's a funny feeling to see a ship you've lived in go like that. It's like some of yourself going down. She reared bow up, slowly, and then started down very gently. The water reached a funnel, which went over with a bang toward the bridge in a shower of sparks. The lieutenant in my boat stood up and called for three cheers for her. Those who could stand up cheered, and I could hear them joining us from the other boats and rafts. Then she was gone.

The lieutenant in my boat, who was the ship's navigator, gave orders to hoist sail, and a few minutes later I heard the captain's boat hailing us, asking our position. I heard it given, and then the captain's voice saying, "In other words, then, we steer east." We went on in an empty sea, with the weather getting worse. All of us were drenched to the skin, but just after midday a Coastal Command airplane appeared, circled over us twice, and then flashed with his Aldis lamp, "Cheer up, there's a destroyer coming."

It arrived, beetling up from the horizon, and I have never seen anything so neat and quick as the way it got us aboard.

Rope ends came down, and the able seamen simply yanked us on deck like fish. The captain was one of the first there, and he stood all the time, still wet and bareheaded, to greet each of us with a word as we boarded. "Glad to see you, Gold," he said to me. The rest was just dry clothes and hot drinks and sleep. But before we went ashore the captain spoke to us all on a last parade, saying what a good ship we had been and how happy he had been. And I remember his last words: "There are six of us who are not here, pray for them as for all good men. And give thanks for your own deliverance."

I Bombed the Ruhr

by an

R.A.F. FLIGHT SERGEANT

IV. I BOMBED THE RUHR

NIGHT after night, bombers of the R.A.F. take off from their bases in Britain to rain destruction on the war factories, ports, railroads, airdromes, and munitions depots of Germany and her occupied territories. Only the end of the war will reveal the real extent of the terrific damage done by Britain's offensive air army. But not even the tight German censorship can conceal the fact that the bombers of the R.A.F. have crippled the German war machine, disrupted communications, and slowed up vital factory production.

The narrator of this story, according to the Air Council's policy, must remain anonymous. He is a twenty-seven-year-old flight sergeant and captain of a twin-engined Handley Page Hampden bomber. He took part in the early "boomphlet" raids—which he now appreciates because of the experience gained in flights over Germany—and has carried out scores of bombing raids on such targets as Kiel, Wilhelmshaven, and the industrial Ruhr.

Member of a service family—his father and brother are also in the R.A.F.—he joined the R.A.F. immediately on leaving school and, after a period of service in India and the Middle East, was picked from the ranks for training as a pilot. He got his "wings" five years ago.

This is his story: I was phoned through to the mess about 6 P.M. to go to operations room, where I got my "Gen" [R.A.F. slang for information, or instructions]. This time, with the other pilots, we were given a squadron target in a Ruhr area which we've visited so often before that I think I could get there blindfolded.

With two other pilots, I shared the great railway marshaling yards at Hamm, filled with war material going to Essen from Hamburg, and barges in the Ems canal near Dortmund. I was also told to take a crack at some oil tanks near a certain river bend at Dortmund. I had a good idea that these tanks had been thoroughly written off on a previous jaunt. If I could make sure this was so, I was allowed to have a go at a chemical factory along toward Duisberg.

After I got my "Gen" I called the three other members of the crew together and we went over the map to decide our route and the order in which we would attack the targets. (We are always allowed a lot of latitude in the choice of routes, because we know by experience what approaches are the best. Jerry is so annoyed about the plastering we've given

48

him recently in this area that he's made some routes very un-
healthy.) Then some of us had a light meal. Personally, I
don't eat at all when I know I'm due for a raid. I find it makes
me sleepy. Nor does my bomb-aimer. But invariably he gets
famished as soon as we've started off and turns his cabin into
a sort of restaurant. We carry rations, of course, mostly fruit
and chocolate, for eating on the homeward journey, and
thermos flasks of either coffee or lemonade.

Just as it was getting dark we boarded the bus and drove
from the airdrome buildings to the "dispersal point," where
our loaded Hampden was waiting. The bomb-aimer and
gunners went to their positions and arranged their gadgets
and guns. I sat about in the cockpit "feeling" myself into my
seat and having a last check-over while the ground crews finished. Then we were off.

I circled the airdrome once or twice, giving everything
another check-over in flight, trying out my controls. Meanwhile the others behind me were gossiping as usual on their
"intercoms" (telephone communications between members
of the crew) or continuing some argument. My bomb-
aimer always grumbles about what a lousy night it is. He
does this no matter how nice a night it is. But he is one of
those funny sort of people who, when they are cheerful, always sound miserable.

After a while the crew went to their positions and we settled down to our job. The night was fine and clear. There

was no moon, and I knew I would have good flying all the way. Heading east, I slowly climbed to 15,000. It was 11 P.M.

Now and then on my intercom I heard little bursts of conversation between the gunners. Mostly they talk about football. Mac is a soccer fan and an ardent follower of the Celtic team. Paddy, on the other hand, cares only for rugby, and thinks soccer is faintly sissy. But the way those two, cooped up in their little gun cabins and peering out into the darkness on these long night flights, have come to reconcile their different passions is a marvel. Neither can see the other. One watches the upper arc and the other the lower. But they work together hand in glove.

I called Taffy, my bomb-aimer, once, but only got a confused mumble in reply. From this, I guessed he was hard at his usual pastime on a raid—eating. Presently the smell of oranges drifting up from his little cabin in front of me confirmed it. I can see him only if I bend forward and peer through a hole under the instrument panel, and then only if enemy searchlights are illuminating his side windows. But I can always tell how far he has got with his repast by the varying smells blown up by the slip-stream draft toward my nostrils. He starts with sardines, goes on to a meat-sandwich snack, usually seasoned with onions, and ends up with oranges and a piece of chocolate.

50

It's a joke between us that one fine night he will fall asleep before we've reached our target. He isn't a very talkative person and sometimes, when he doesn't answer quickly enough through the intercom, I fire a burst from my front gun—just for the hell of it. "What the devil's that?" he bawls crossly through the phones. "Oh, I thought you were asleep," I reply blandly.

Holland was dark as we approached, the flat shore and the sea merging into one. I thought how, only a few weeks ago, when we used to pass it well off on our right on our way toward Heligoland Bight to break into northern Germany, it was a blaze of light. Now it seemed darker and emptier even than blacked-out England. It had a "dead" look, even from 17,000 feet in the night sky.

Far up to the north toward the Bight and "Windy Corner," which I had got to know so well, the sky was alight with bursting A.A., searchlights, and tracers, which told me that some of the other boys were already livening up Kiel a bit. I flew in over Holland, heading for the objective.

To the left and right a group of searchlights swung up and felt about for me. They were well away, but I "de-sinked" [de-synchronized] my motors just to baffle the sound locators a bit. Abruptly the searchlights joined together, lingered for a moment, and then went out.

We rode on, the motors roaring sweetly in the darkness. I

called down through the intercom, checking my compass bearing and other instruments with Taffy. A bank of clouds began to form 6,000 feet below. And then more searchlights came up ahead, making the cloud formation a beautiful, shimmering floor of light. I had just passed over this area feeling hidden and secure when I heard Paddy calling to Mac from the lower gun position.

"Six fighters below. . . . M.E.'s, I think. . . . They're coming up fast. Come on, you so-and-so's," Mac called back, asking where and what range. Paddy said they were about 800 yards away and well below on the right beam. He could see them quite well, silhouetted against the lit clouds. And they could see us, no doubt. I banked and swung a bit to give Mac, in his upper position, a peep and a chance to level his guns.

I could hear Paddy whistling through his teeth as he squinted along his sights, and then a groaning, cursing dialogue between the pair of them.

"They won't come in, the dirty so-and-so's," Paddy fumed. And Mac, shouting as if the M.E.'s could hear, "Come on, come on, and take a crack." But the M.E.'s didn't. They stayed well out of range until we lost them.

But by now I had plenty of other things to think about. We were just picking up the edge of the Rhine, and clouds below were thickening. Calling back, I told them all to watch for a turn in the river and a certain group of bridges which would give an approach line on our first objective.

I throttled back to come down to 2,000 feet for the identification run in. Down we went with feathered screws, and then through the cloud layer. And there below, faintly lit by the moon, was the bend in the river. I saw it the same instant that Taffy and the two gunners called out. Banking steeply and hauling the control column back into my stomach, I shot up to about 8,000 feet again, over the bridges which would give us our line. But we could have got along without the help of any of these identification marks. As usual, Jerry lit up our target for us. The whole of Duisberg was ablaze with searchlights, tracers, "flaming onions" [big globes of greenish-colored fire linked together in groups of about eight], and some stuff I had never seen before. It was a white, shiny substance, looking something like Christmas-tree tinsel. We watched it for a while as I climbed to 12,000 feet, circling along the outside of the searchlights and all the muck [gunfire] that was coming up.

The white fiery stuff seemed to drift lazily about the sky. It was very beautiful, but somehow very sinister. I didn't like it a bit. I heard Paddy saying to Mac, conversationally, "That looks lovely a long way off, doesn't it?" And Taffy broke off from chanting the course changes to add, "Yes, a *bloody* long way off. As far as possible suits me."

The sky in front and over our objectives was so full of bursting A.A. that I could hear the detonations even above the roar of our motors. There was real hell to pay. And I could see the reason for it. Far below and ahead I could see flashes caused by bombs from other aircraft of our squadron. A fire had already started somewhere in the factory buildings. The German batteries and A.A. groups were apparently too busy with other chaps of ours at work upstairs to spot me, however. I kept circling well to the outside and waited till the bomb flashes stopped.

Then I called through the intercom to the crew that we were now going in to take a crack at them. I throttled back and shoved the nose down. Taffy got me dead on the line to the target. Down we went toward the muck. The altimeter needle began to fly round—6,000, 5,000, 4,000. The wind screamed past the throttled motors, and then we were in the midst of all the gunfire. The racket was terrific. Tracers were swinging past the windows as the guns below hose-piped across our path. Short-range A.A. shells were bursting under the aircraft, bucketing us about. All the time Taffy was holding me on the line. "Right a bit . . . steady . . . Left a bit . . . steady." At about 1,000 feet I started to level out. I pulled the bomb-selection levers, ready for Taffy to press the button. That same instant the searchlights got us. I bent low to keep the glare from my eyes, and fixed them on the instrument dials. Through the hole beneath the panel I got a momentary glimpse of the back of Taffy's head, intent on the bomb sights and black against the glare lighting up his cabin. Then the ship gave a great swinging lift upward, and I knew the first lot of bombs had gone. At the same instant a group of A.A. shell bursting below almost flung us on our back. The blast was a sheer physical shock like a bang on the back of the head. I did not know if we had been hit, but I fought her back level again, the motors roaring evenly, although everything was dancing on the instrument panel.

The gunners behind had their eyes glued on the ground, spotting our bomb bursts. A second or so later, though it seemed long minutes, Paddy bawled through the intercom, "Off right." Taffy's line could not have been so good after all—or else that shell salvo might have thrown us off at the moment of release. I slid through the muck, adopting violent avoiding action, but I could not throw off the searchlights. Nothing hit us however, and, keeping on, I lost the lights.

I turned and started to come in again to make a proper job of it this time. Taffy got on his line and then we were in the midst of the muck again. Flaming onions curled past on each side, lighting up the whole cabin with their green glow. There was a colossal burst on my starboard side and the intercom to the bomb-aimer broke down. All I could do was to hold her dead on the last compass reading and chance it. From this new approach the target was now clearly visible to me. I could even see the girders of the factory outlined against the fire within.

Then came the great lift again as the second lot of bombs went. I banked steeply to watch, as the searchlights had either lost me or were put out. I could hear Paddy's and Mac's guns clattering away, shooting down the beams at the great lenses below.

There was no mistake about this stick of bombs. I saw the flash of their bursts, and then a great, billowing greenish explosion. A second or so later a terrific air blast reached us, flinging us completely on our back this time. The panel lights went out. The next seconds were hell and confusion. I had not the foggiest notion how I was flying or whether I was heading for the deck or not. I called through the intercom to the rest to prepare to bale out, but my mouth and throat were so dry that I could only whisper. They never heard me —not that it would have been much good, anyway, at our height.

All the time I was fighting the controls. For one moment I thought the ailerons had gone, but then suddenly I saw the glare and flashes below swing past my windows in a great arc, and I knew I was flying level. The panel lights were still out, but I used the flames of the burning factory and oil tanks at Duisberg as a sort of horizon.

Gradually things sorted themselves. Taffy came through on the intercom. He had been almost knocked out by ammunition drums which had come adrift and hit him as we turned

over. The gunners were all right, though they had had a lot
of nasty bumps. Hampdens are not exactly adapted for flying on their backs. Taffy was quite calm, however, and it was
nice hearing his grumbling voice again, asking me if I wanted
a bearing for our next target—the railway marshaling yards
beyond Essen. I called him up from his bomb-aiming cabin
to do something about my panel lights, because I could not
fiddle with the broken connections from my seat. The lights
came on and I set the course for the railway yards. Taffy
grinned up at me and jabbed his thumbs up before he went
back to his position.

It was now 1 A.M., and I realized with a shock that we had
only been an hour over Duisberg. It seemed a year. We went
on, the motors pulling serenely away in a wide sweep around
Essen. I could see there was a spot of bother going on there
too, but Essen was not my pigeon that night, so I gave it a
wide berth. Searchlights came up again, held us, and lost us.
On our way to Hamm and the Dortmund-Ems canal corner
we went through an almost continual curtain of muck. I
swung from side to side between the tracer streamers and
the flaming onions which seemed to curl round us continually but never touched. My eyes were getting tired with the
searchlight glare and the strain of watching the instrument
board. I hoped that Taffy was all right and kept calling him
to make sure. I knew that the gunners were all right—Mac

was actually yarning to Paddy about some salmon-poaching he had done in Scotland. God knows what had reminded him of that. I expect they were both a bit bored. No fighters had come near us since the bunch by the Rhine.

Then the railway yards came in sight. Leaning out of my window, I could see all the tracks running together at a junction and a lot of wagons on the tracks. They were there quite plainly at 4,000 feet. The muck started to come up again, but I cared less this time. Keeling over, I came down in a great dive to about 1,000 feet and blasted through it. I threw the bomb-selector over for the last stick. Taffy was on the line right away, and a second later the last one dropped away. They were flush hits, all bunched dead on the rail junction and a line of trucks.

I kept going down, turned, and at less than 300 feet ran in to have a good look at what damage we had done. At that height the A.A. guns could not get on to us, and we roared across the target. A rail shed was on fire, tracks were burst apart, and just as we passed the trucks some of them went up. I grabbed the column back quickly, since the blast shoved us on our nose, but it was not as bad this time as over Duisberg.

There was no point in looking at Dortmund, because we had used our bomb ration in making sure of the target at Duisberg. Banging the throttle open, I went upstairs then and headed for home.

Convoy

by

ALLAN A. MICHIE

V. CONVOY

WEEK after week, the men of the destroyers, corvettes, sloops, and armed trawlers—the little vessels of the British Navy—push out from the ports of Britain on convoy patrol duty. To these men of the Royal Navy, facing the dangers of lurking U-boats, the fierce storms and icy cold of the Atlantic are just part of a routine job. It is an unheralded job, carried out in utmost secrecy, with few occasions for dramatic heroism, but it is a job as important to Britain's war effort as the exploits of the R.A.F. in the skies. Without these men, and the cargoes they bring safely into port, Britons would starve, factories would cease producing.

To these men, this story is dedicated.

Aboard an M-Class 1,500-ton British destroyer I sailed from a port on the west coast of Britain for a week's patrol duty escorting convoys along the Atlantic sea-lanes. Our outward-bound convoy had been passing slowly downriver all morning, and the vessels were moving off in column formation from the estuary as we caught up with them. There were twenty-one vessels in line—seven more were to join us later from another port—and they flew many flags: six were Norwegians, two Dutch, two smelly Greek tramps, one a spanking, white-painted Swede, and the rest British.

With a corvette, a fast little naval auxiliary vessel which formed part of the convoy escort, we shuttled behind and around the columns, herding stragglers into line. From the destroyer's bridge the captain, a friendly faced young man who had taken his ship and his boys safely through the Dunkirk show, shouted instructions through the loudspeaker to each vessel: "Come on there, Number 34! Pull up your socks! This is your last chance to catch up with the convoy. . . . Number 26, you're out of position already."

Safely in the middle of the convoy we could see three liners carrying evacuated children, two bound for Montreal, one for South Africa. As we raced past one, the youngsters, each with a lifebelt on, crowded to the rail, and three hundred little voices sang out with "There'll Always Be an England!" With lumps in our throats we said silent prayers that nothing would happen to *them* during the journey.

Each merchant convoy is commanded by a commodore, a retired admiral recalled for wartime duty. He sets the speed and the course of the convoy, but as long as the escort vessels are with his convoy his orders are subject to the approval of the senior officer in charge of the escort vessels, who is usually of a much lower rank, at most a destroyer commander. The active destroyer officers good-naturedly let the admirals have their own way most of the time, but when one gets particularly sticky they delight in letting him know who's boss. Back in port, at the hotel where I had spent the night before sailing, the naval boys around the bar were still chuckling about the old admiral who had been "throwing his weight about" and had snubbed an escorting commanding officer on an outward trip. A few weeks later, on an inward-bound voyage, the officer had the misfortune to pick up a convoy under the same admiral. It had been a filthy night, and as convoy and escort met in the fog at their Atlantic rendezvous an order flashed out from the admiral's vessel: "Count my convoy," it said, without as much as a please.

Back flashed the escort commander: "Sorry. I'm not good at arithmetic!"

We knew that we had a good chance of running into trouble before we were more than half a day out of port. A wireless message informed us that two freighters had been torpedoed by U-boats and that a number of German submarines were lying in their favorite spots along the Atlantic sea routes. The weather promised to be bad, and didn't wait long in living up to it. Just as we left the estuary an incoming destroyer passed close enough for us to see that two of her life-boats had been crushed on their davits by the rough seas. With her Aldis lamp she flashed word that the night before a huge wave had swept her gunnery officer into the sea. Another wave had washed him back onto the deck, tearing off his right ear in the process. A gale had been blowing for ten days, and a good deal of winter weather remained for us.

A destroyer 300 feet long and 30 feet wide is not the steadiest vessel on the seas, and for two days out of the seven I was aboard it was so rough that it was risky to walk along the narrow decks. We had to sleep in our clothes for seven days, with deflated lifebelts constantly around our chests. I have never been more than a moderately good sailor, and the mere thought of a trip aboard a destroyer into the Atlantic made me feel squeamish before my train had left London. But one doesn't refuse an Admiralty invitation to go out on the Atlantic Patrol. With a reporter representing the United Press, I was sharing the honor of being the first American correspondent allowed to cover the activities of convoy escort vessels in the Atlantic.

Our outward trip was quiet enough. On the second day out a wireless message came through saying that a lone freighter had been torpedoed about sixty miles ahead of us. A few hours later we came upon her, still afloat, although the torpedo had torn a gaping hole in her prow. The crew had taken to the boats and were nowhere in sight on the rolling seas, but a fishing drifter had spotted the damaged vessel, and its crew of five were struggling hard to get a line aboard her. It seemed an impossible job for a tiny fishing boat to tow a good-sized freighter back to port, so the destroyer's captain shouted through the loudspeaker that he would wireless for a couple of tugs to pull her to Belfast. But the men on the drifter wouldn't hear of it. They had found the freighter first. If they managed to get her into port, their salvage reward would come to about £5,000 each, more than they could earn in years of fishing. We left them still trying to clamber up the freighter's sides and make fast their lines.

Next day we had a report that a German bomber had attacked another merchantman a hundred miles away from us, and our gun crews stayed hopefully at their stations all day, but we had no luck. The only planes we saw on the outward voyage were British—Ansons, Stranraers, and huge Short Sunderland flying boats, which cruised around and around our convoy, keeping a sharp eye for underwater shadows indicating U-boats.

At the end of the fourth day out we left our outward convoy and moved off northward to pick up the inward-bound vessels coming from New York and Montreal, which we were scheduled to meet at a rendezvous early next morning. That day broke with a pea-soup fog and the convoy nowhere in sight. We zigzagged back and forth along the course we thought it should have taken, but since we hadn't had a sight at the sun ourselves for two days, we weren't even sure of our own position. It wasn't until the fog had lifted at four that afternoon that we sighted the vessels on the horizon ahead. It was a big convoy. Through the glasses as we came up fast behind them I counted forty-five vessels; ironically, five of them flying the British flag were captured German merchantmen converted for service in the British merchant marine. I could see American-made trucks, ambulances, and massive airplane crates lashed on their decks.

Just before dusk the destroyer's crew were piped to their practice action stations. Up on the bridge, as the captain and navigator handled the rolling ship, the No. 1 officer marked out practice orders to his gun crews: "Exercise alarm, starboard, bearing green sixty. . . . Target, a battleship . . . range one hundred and thirty-nine . . . deflection fourteen left . . . rate four hundred . . . right four. . . . Salvos! . . . Open fire! . . . Shoot! . . . Left eight. . . . Shoot! . . . Target bearing amidships. . . . All guns check, check, check!"

The captain broke in to say that a wireless message advised him to alter course because there was a submarine twenty miles ahead. Before the words were out of his mouth there came a terrific explosion which shook the whole convoy.

66

CONVOY

CONVOY AT DUSK ON THE ATLANTIC

RUNNING THE GANTLET

CAPTAIN WILLIAM HENRY DAWSON, M.B.E.

RUNNING THE GANTLET

THE "JOHN M'S" GUNNERS

CABLE 1301

WALTER GRAEBNER   ALLAN A. MICHIE

"UP PERISCOPE!"

BRITISH SUBMARINE IN PORT

"UP PERISCOPE!"

LOADING TORPEDO

OUR HOUSE WAS BOMBED

MRS. LILIAN MARGARET HART AND HER HOME

OUR HOUSE WAS BOMBED

END OF BOMBING

"Twenty miles ahead, hell," snapped the captain. "It's right here!" The stern of the last vessel on the outside column away from us reared into the air, then settled back on the water. The rest of the convoy automatically changed course and veered away from the scene, leaving the fastest merchantman to pick up the survivors. We raced to the spot where the captain estimated the torpedo had been fired from.

It was blowing furiously; mountainous waves cascaded up over the bow, even over the towering bridge, and the vessel tossed about like a cork. Every time we made a sharp turn, the destroyer heeled over until the deck rails plowed up the water and those of us on deck had to hang onto the lifelines around the gun turrets to avoid going overboard. Although we shuttled back and forth for two hours, the destroyer's Asdic (Britain's hush-hush weapon, named after the Anti-Submarine Detection Investigation Committee, which has provided a surefire method of locating U-boats) could pick up no trace of this one, and reluctantly we pushed on to take up position at the rear of the convoy for the all-night patrol.

In port a few days later, I collected the German communiqués issued during the week; the one announcing the attack on our convoy was a perfect example of how the Nazis are achieving their "successes" at sea against Britain. The merchantman we'd lost—incidentally, the first lost by my destroyer in ten months of convoy-escort work, which made the officers and crew pretty downhearted—was a 5,000-ton freighter. Five members of the crew had been killed outright when the torpedo exploded, but the remaining twenty-six had been hauled aboard the rescue vessel. The communiqué, issued by the German High Command, boosted this little freighter into three vessels totaling 29,000 tons, including one 12,000-ton tanker.

The morning after the attack broke clear and fine, and I moved onto the aft deck and squatted under the gun muzzle reading *Kitty Foyle*. The seas had lessened into the long Atlantic swell, and the convoy zigzagged majestically onward. Except for the gun over my head and the deadly cylindrical depth charges lying in rows just beyond my feet, I might have been on a peacetime crossing of the Atlantic.

Suddenly the lookout near me gave a startled shout. A "tin fish" (torpedo) nosed past us 50 feet astern and headed straight into the convoy! With hearts in our mouths, we waited helplessly for the explosion as it passed into the first column of unsuspecting vessels. There was no time to warn them, and it would have been useless for the whole convoy to alter course or stop. It seemed that we stood waiting at the rails for hours. We couldn't believe that a torpedo could pass through forty-five vessels without a hit, yet, miraculously, nothing happened! Then a signal light flashed out from the corvette patrolling the far side of the convoy: "Torpedo passed 20 feet astern apparently near end of run."

Leaving the corvette to shepherd the convoy off in the opposite direction, the officers on the destroyer's bridge quickly worked out the probable position of the U-boat. The "tin fish" had been fired quite a distance to port of us. We revved up to the limit and raced to the spot, with the Asdic sounding. Just as the Asdic picked up confirmation that the U-boat was near us, another torpedo passed us astern and headed off into the empty sea. Instead of diving for the bottom, the U-boat had stayed near the surface to take another crack at us.

As we slowed down to work out the U-boat's exact position, the Short Sunderland which had been patrolling over the convoy came roaring overhead and plunked a smoke float onto the water about 300 feet to starboard of us. Wheeling quickly back over the float, it dropped one bomb on a long, dark shadow just under the water. "Submarine submerging," flashed out on the Aldis lamp in the Sunderland's cabin.

"Stand by depth charges!" shouted the captain on the destroyer's bridge.

"Stand by depth charges!" echoed the gunnery officer, standing aft with his men. The destroyer's engines strained and we headed straight for the spot where the bomb had dropped. Just at this moment the wardroom steward, unable to stay below any longer for fear of missing the fun and games, dashed out on deck and handed me my lunch—poached eggs on toast. Buzzers sounded on the aft deck, and overboard went a pattern of depth charges. In a few seconds came the almost simultaneous explosions, a huge column of water spouted high in the air, the destroyer's stern lifted slightly out of the water and shook violently, and my two poached eggs went bouncing off the plate onto the deck.

Slewing around without a stop, we dropped more drums of TNT on the same spot. When the water had stilled we could still pick up the sound of the U-boat on the bottom. The first pattern of charges had knocked out the destroyer's buzzer system, so we stood off at a distance to repair it and hoist new charges on the throwers. As we waited, the Sunderland roared back for its crack. Three bombs came tumbling from its belly and went plummeting below the surface. Again the destroyer picked up the U-boat's presence on the bottom.

Our engines strained again and we rushed in for another attack: a second pattern went overboard and exploded close to the bottom of the sea. Hundreds of fish, stunned by the explosion, floated belly-up to the surface. When the water had stilled we cruised slowly over the spot. There was no trace of the U-boat in the Asdic. As we waited hopefully, huge quantities of oil floated to the surface and spread out thickly over the water. Officers and men aboard the destroyer broke into a cheer, and as the Sunderland slid over just above our heads the pilot gave us the "thumbs up" victory sign. That night we broke wireless silence to send a message to the naval authorities ashore saying that Britain had one less U-boat to worry about.

Next morning we herded the convoy through the North Channel between Ireland and the tip of Kintyre, off the Scottish coast. In the clouds above we could hear a German bomber shuttling back and forth over our convoy, and our gun crews stood waiting expectantly for the attack. But before we could get in a shot, three Hurricanes beetled out from land, and that was the last we heard of the German.

In one week we had convoyed seventy-three merchantmen with the loss of one. In the Irish Sea we passed another outward convoy of fifty-one vessels nosing steadily toward the Atlantic, and still more columns of freighters were assembling in the estuary as we maneuvered our charges into port. As we tied up alongside the oiler I saw through the glasses a wharf piled high with huge wooden packing cases. Across each case were stenciled the words BRITAIN DELIVERS THE GOODS, the new slogan of the export-conscious British Board of Trade. Watching the cases being slung aboard a waiting freighter, it wasn't hard to conclude that Germany's proclaimed "complete blockade of Britain" is a Goebbelsesque invention compounded of wishful thinking and pure poppycock.

Running the Gantlet

by

CAPTAIN WILLIAM HENRY DAWSON, M.B.E.

VI. RUNNING THE GANTLET

THE German claim that occupation of France gave them control of Britain's vital sea-lane, the English Channel, has been turned into a hollow boast by the hardihood of heroic merchant sailors like the narrator of this story. Captain William Henry Dawson, forty-two-year-old veteran of the World War and master of the 500-ton coaster *John M.* of London, is only one of many dogged Britons engaged in the important coastal traffic which, despite Nazi E-boats (fast German motor torpedo boats; "E" is British for "Enemy"), dive bombers, and long-range guns, run regularly between north and south of Britain.

This is Dawson's story: It was about 1:30 A.M. in the morning of August 8, 1940, when the first enemy attack came—the worst I have had to go through in this war and the beginning of a harrowing twelve-hour ordeal that nearly finished my ship and almost settled me as well.

The night was fine and clear but black as pitch. Hanging

75

to the rail on the bridge of the *John M.*, I hoped the fresh air would help keep me awake after twenty-four hours on deck. Loaded with coal from the north, we had come down the Thames Estuary and through Dover Straits. Now we were running west, roughly off Newhaven on the coast of Sussex, in a convoy flanked by armed trawlers and vessels dragging barrage balloons overhead.

There had been some fun and games earlier that evening off Dover. Nothing serious—just a few dive bombers which were broken up by R.A.F. fighters before they could get really going. But coming on top of five dive bombings in a fortnight, added to the growing strain of long hours on watch in these Channel runs, it had been enough to get me feeling tensed up. Still, I thought, the darkness would give us a few hours of peace from the Germans.

Then, suddenly, I saw a blinding flash, followed by a heavy explosion in the starboard column of the convoy. A second later the same thing happened out in the port column. The explosions, distant as they were, rocked the ship, and I could smell the cordite fumes blown over on the wind.

"What the hell's happening now?" I thought. Although it took me some seconds to grasp the meaning of it, I instantly told the helmsman to swing out starboard four points, port four points, zigzagging against submarines. I hung over the bridge straining to see into the blackness around, hoping to

God I wouldn't run into the ships ahead and abeam, hoping they were zigzagging too.

When I heard the roar of motor engines away to beam, I guessed what was up. E-boats! In the same second flares exploded overhead, and I heard the scream of aero-engines zooming upward. In the white glare I saw the whole convoy scattered over the sea and noted at the same time that I had plenty of room. In the same instant I could see my gun crews running to stations fore, aft, and amidships, all in a mad sort of panorama. And then the flares went out. I rang down for more of my engines. Just then Very lights, fired from the E-boats, curved up from the darkness to port and starboard, and the next second the guard boats went into action. They had seen the E-boats at last, and the whole line on either side flickered with gun flashes, although from my position in the center column I could still see nothing of the enemy. We zigzagged crazily on.

More Very lights came up, illuminating the whole expanse of the convoy again. There was another huge explosion astern, and the gunfire mounted higher. I saw one of the convoy ships, astern in the pallid glare from a clump of drooping Verys, slowly rearing bow upward out of the water. As she sank, I counted the black specks sliding down boat-falls into the water. These were the survivors.

As the Verys went out, searchlights swung across the water,

and in that instant I saw an E-boat quite plainly, right on my starboard beam and less than three hundred yards away. My Lewis gun on top of the bridge went into action. Spouts of water plumped round it—shellfire from the invisible guard-ships. I saw the E-boat for a second or two longer, heeling over in a great smother of white foam as she swung about and tore off again at something over thirty knots. Then the search-lights lost her and she escaped into the covering darkness.

We plunged on, the racket now dying down a bit. I signaled my ship's number to the convoy commodore and got the flash of his acknowledgment. The gunfire was now ebbing away astern, where I could see the glare from a burning ship among the gun flashes. We got the order to close up a bit. It was now 2:30 A.M.

I was just drinking some coffee which the cook had brewed for the crew when I heard the sound of aircraft overhead again. Down came the flares lighting us up, then the clatter of machine-gun fire. I just glimpsed the flash of tracer bullets streaking into the sea ahead of us when I heard the whistle of a bomb. It struck the water about fifty yards abeam. The explosion seemed to lift my ship up bodily and drop it again. It flung the coffee cup out of my hand and knocked me flying into the opposite corner of the bridge. My head bashed into an iron stanchion, and I saw more stars than there were in the heavens. I thought all the teeth in my head had become unshipped. While I lay there for a second or two gathering my wits together, my Lewis gunners went into action against one aircraft which had dived under the flares. I picked myself up as all hell was breaking loose again. The E-boats were coming in for a second and bigger attack, helped by the flares from the aircraft overhead, which were lighting up the whole convoy.

While I was lying there, half stunned in the corner of the bridge, the mate, who was in the wheelhouse, had already swung the ship into a zigzag. I went back to my station in the starboard corner and watched. This time the E-boats were not finding it so easy. The sea around was alive with searchlights and the guard-ships were pumping star shells as well as high explosives into the water all around when suddenly I saw an E-boat again on my beam, traveling parallel with my course and not many yards away. My gunners saw it at the same time and, although it seemed to be just a swiftly moving streak of white foam, they poured at least a couple of drums of ammunition into it before it swung over and vanished. I am certain we hit it.

Sometime in the middle of it all I peered through the protection slit of the wheelhouse at the clock. It was 3:30 A.M. Only two hours had gone by since the first attack. It seemed like two years.

When the bombers had gone, I started along the decks on

a tour of inspection. There seemed to be no damage so far, and the gunners were cheerful and ready at their posts. The three gunners whom we coasters always pick up when we run the gantlet of the Dover Straits were a bit sore, however, because they had not had much of a chance for a shoot, and they envied the men on the outside columns of the convoy. That last E-boat gave us our only chance, and one of my own A.B. gunners had got that with the Lewis gun on top of the wheelhouse.

With the first light of dawn I saw that I was practically alone. The rest of the convoy were scattered specks along the horizon. E-boats and aircraft had disappeared, but there was plenty to do for the next few hours. I slowed down while the stragglers in the convoy were brought in. I was kept busy answering and acting on signals, while the naval craft scurried around doing their famous dog act, gathering the convoy back into formation. Then I grabbed breakfast and took a quick shave to brace me up.

At 11:30 A.M. I went round for another look over my ship. Everything was quiet. We were off St. Catherine's Point on the Isle of Wight, and the convoy had closed in to within sight of the land, less than four miles away. A few minutes later the peace was broken with a terrific explosion right ahead of us. I dashed onto the bridge, picked up my glasses, and saw shells from shore batteries plunging into the sea ahead and around racing peaks of foam. E-boats again, but this time they were heading for the French coast. No doubt their purpose was to give away the position of our convoy to the dive bombers.

I guessed we were soon in for another dose, and I was not long in doubt. Just after midday I saw a balloon coming down in flames ahead of us, followed by bomb thuds on the distant horizon. I called the men to action stations, and swung out to starboard on the first leg of a zigzag.

Then I saw them—flocks of dive bombers under the high cloud, racing toward my section of the convoy. They came along in V formation, and then flicked into the old familiar "line ahead" position for the attack. Down they came. I could hear the scream of the leader's flight above the rattle of my guns, which had already opened up. I saw the bombs leave and hurtle downward. The first salvo hit a Norwegian ship on my starboard side. I saw the plumes of smoke and the big columns of sea water rise up as they struck on and near her.

On we went, zigzagging madly. Up went the Jerries into the clouds, and down came the second batch. This salvo missed us by about a hundred yards, and they must have all been duds. Hanging onto the bridge rail, and holding my breath, I watched them plummet straight at us from where the dive bombers had pulled out four hundred feet up. I followed them down with my eyes and saw them hit the water and bounce out again. One of them bounced twice. They were screaming bombs, but they didn't explode. Perhaps the screaming gadget —the whistle or whatever it is that they have fixed on their fins—might have put them off their course. Away to starboard another flight was diving down. I watched still another bunch forming in line ahead, and down they came. Swallowing hard, I saw them come, and out of the corner of my eye I saw my gun crews flinging in drums. Then this salvo crashed. The first one hit the water near the starboard bow, the other was a near-miss amidships. Again we experienced the familiar feeling of the ship being lifted and dropped. Down came more bombs, flinging up great columns of water nearly one hundred feet high, which plunged over the ship and drenched all of us.

I saw one water column, green between me and the sun, smash over the forecastle head and sweep the two gunners off their feet. Ahead to port I saw a bomb hit the commodore's ship and set it on fire. Down came more stuff, and at one time at least twenty bombs struck on either side. The ship heaved wildly and guns flashed out all round the convoy. In the middle of the party the mate dashed into the wheelhouse, shoved the man away from the wheel, and shouted, "For God's sake, let me do *something*."

There was another screaming dive out of the clouds. This salvo was nearest of all. It turned the ship nearly over on her beam ends. She righted slowly and shuddered. Then there was a crash below, and the engines stopped. We lost way and swung round in a long curve.

"Now we're finished," I thought. The Junkers were re-forming again and we were just a helpless sitter. They came down, but to another part of the convoy. They were all misses. Two of the Junkers broke up in tatters, hit during the dive by ship fire.

I turned round in the middle of the din and found the chief engineer at my elbow. He was drenched to the skin from the water which had plunged down into the engine room. But he grinned at me, and then reported that the main engines were gone and the auxiliaries had been smashed by the bomb concussions. "She's making water," he said, "and I'm afraid we're going to lose her."

I ordered away the lifeboat, which is always hung over the side in readiness while we are running in convoy, and the men began to go to the boat station. But as the boat touched the water, she began to fill. She had been holed by bomb splinters or by E-boat fire the night before. There was nothing to be done except signal the escort vessels. It was then only about 12:30 P.M. Dazedly, I was trying to reconcile myself to the loss of my ship and wondering what to do. The Junkers were still raising hell and every ship in the convoy was in action. I was dropping slowly behind as the convoy steamed on.

Then, from the Lewis gunner on the monkey island above the wheelhouse, I heard a shout: "Here come the Spitfires!" I turned my head toward the land and saw a whole squadron of them coming glinting out of the sun and heard the scream of their supercharged engines going full out even above the noise of the gunfire. In they came bald-headed at the Junker squadrons, which were just forming up for a mass dive. It was the grandest sight I have ever seen. For the next few seconds the sky was simply full of whirling aircraft and falling, flaming black streaks of crashing dive bombers which had set out to massacre our convoy. It was all over in a few minutes. The sky was clear now except for the Spitfires, which had come down and were roaring and circling over our head.

During this last minute or two I had heard a lot of banging down below, and the second mate came up to me with a message from the chief to say that although the auxiliaries were smashed and their bedplates gone, they could manage to repair the main engines and thus keep the pumps going. There was some hope that we might make port. I signaled the escort vessels that I would try to make Poole Harbor, or otherwise try to beach her, and asked one of the escort vessels to stand by us. We got under way again, limping along toward the shore. Behind me I could see boats standing by a sinking vessel and the commodore's ship, which was still on fire.

Halfway to shore, more Junkers appeared in the distance,

even more than had attacked us the first time. There were German fighters with them, and the Spitfire squadron shot upward into action. More Spitfires came out from the land, and a terrific fight took place over our heads. At one time I counted nearly two hundred aircraft in action. In a quarter of an hour's progress toward the land, I saw twelve machines coming down in flames, ten of them dive bombers. And to the running accompaniment of this battle overhead we made our way, leaking like a basket from broken rivets and battered plates. Toward the end of that half-hour, the escort vessel signaled asking if I could still keep water down in my holds and make for Weymouth. This we eventually did. After repairs and a much-needed overhaul, we were out running the Channel gantlet again. It has got to be done, dive bombers or no dive bombers, blockade or no blockade, and we're the boys to do it.

Since this chapter was written, Captain Dawson has been awarded the M.B.E., and his chief engineer, Harold George Travis, and gunner, Robert Daniel Thomas, commended for the action described in the story.

Cable 1301

by

ALLAN A. MICHIE

and

WALTER GRAEBNER

VII. CABLE 1301

IN THE evening of September 18, 1940, a crippled Nazi Junkers bomber, hit repeatedly by anti-aircraft fire as it attempted to raid the center of London, sailed silently into an unsuspecting Bloomsbury square. At least one bomb exploded in its rack as the plane was above the square, and a land mine aboard blew up with a terrific explosion as the plane crashed, leveling several houses, setting fire to others. Two American war correspondents were in their house, a few doors away, when the plane crashed. This is the story they cabled to America:

GRAEBNER: At a quarter to eight I left the *Daily Express* morgue, where I'd been gathering material on Prime Minister Churchill. My taxi whizzed recklessly through the darkened streets because the driver wanted to be out of Central London before the sirens wailed. I was just eating my dinner of lamb chops and baked beans—cooked on an electric fireplace since our gas supply had gone—when the raid started. The drone of German planes, clatter of anti-aircraft muck, the whistling and thuds of bombs grew so loud that I decided it was time to drift down to the basement, where we had improvised a shelter in a dirty wine cellar. I quickly changed into pajamas, flannel trousers, and tweed jacket, grabbed the portable radio and my typewriter, and hurried down four floors. We lived in a charming seventeenth-century brownstone house in a quiet London square. The house was occupied by the Charles Laughtons until the war started. Laughton and wife, Elsa Lanchester, had spent a few thousand pounds modernizing it, and we certainly didn't want anything to happen to it.

MICHIE: I had dropped into a newsreel theater in the late afternoon to see a couple of Donald Duck cartoons in order to break the monotony of two weeks of almost continuous air raids, and decided to eat dinner in the West End instead of going home. I was just dawdling over my omelet and a half-bottle of lovely Sauterne when the waiter announced that the nightly Mona [the warning: the all-clear is Clara] had gone, a little earlier than usual. By the time I had finished dinner and started homeward the air was thick with muck, and the ack ack flashes were so bright I could almost read my paper. It's almost impossible to get taxis during raids, so I didn't waste time trying but hurried in the direction of our house in a half-walk, half-run, popping into doorways for a second whenever the stuff burst overhead. Londoners call this mode of travel door-hopping! I remember stopping outside a Lyons Corner House to buy a late paper, and was so amazed at the sight of an old newsboy calmly sitting selling his papers with a sky full of shrapnel that I gave him a sixpence for a penny paper.

Just as I reached our square the sky on my right suddenly lighted up in a bright-red glow. Then came a terrific explosion. I was smack in the open, without a sheltering doorway to pop into, so I just stood still. Nothing fell around me, so I raced for our home. Inside I found Graebner in the shelter and our housekeeper on the point of going out to meet her husband, who is quartered in London on army duty. My description of the fun and games outside quickly changed her mind. As soon as there came a lull in the ack ack fire, I raced upstairs to change into old clothes for shelter sleeping, and she followed to telephone her husband.

GRAEBNER: I had just comfortably propped myself up against pillows on top of a mattress and was listening to the nine-o'clock news on the radio in my lap when there came a deafening crash which made me think that my world had come to an end. I could hear debris falling all over the place, but mainly above me, and an instant later the ceiling of the basement started cracking and bits of plaster cascaded to the floor. I was sure the whole house was coming down and would be on top of me before I could escape. I was absolutely certain that Michie and the housekeeper were either dead or seriously injured.

For a few seconds I was too stunned to move. Then I remembered that I'd better clap on my steel helmet, but I was so jittery I couldn't find it for a minute. I groped in the brick cubicles of the wine vault over and over when I suddenly discovered I had had it in my hand all the time. Before going upstairs I decided to check on the two basement exits. If the upper part of the house was a shambles or aflame I wanted to be sure that I could get out from the cellar. The front basement door was still intact, but it was locked and I had no key. I rushed through to the back door, but when I opened it clouds of dust and the burnt smell of exploded bombs burst in and almost suffocated me. I slammed the door and raced upstairs, thinking that the worst had happened but praying hard for the best. I wrenched open the door to the main floor passage and shouted, "Allan . . . Helene." The male and female "We're all right" that answered me were the six sweetest words I've ever heard.

MICHIE: I had changed into old trousers, wool shirt, and leather jacket, and was just standing in the fourth-floor bathroom when, without the usual bomb-swishing sound of warning, there came a terrific explosion in the square at the front of the house. I stood transfixed as the whole house swayed crazily from side to side. My brain kept shouting, "Get downstairs before the next one drops," but for some strange reason I persisted in going through the mechanical motions of flushing the toilet, buttoning my trousers, and putting out the bathroom light before I finally jumped and ran down to the third floor. I grabbed my typewriter and some paper from the hall table, and remember hearing the housekeeper cry over the phone to her husband, "Something's happening to our house. I've got to go." Before she could hang up the receiver the second explosion came. The blast blew in the hall window and the blackout paper wrapped itself around me as I was blown rump over teakettle into the kitchen, falling over Graebner's cocker spaniel Bepi and my typewriter on the way. The housekeeper was blown into the dining room as its windows came tumbling down, and the electric fireplace was flung across into the bookcase on the other side of the room. Furniture in both rooms went toppling crazily backward, and a heavy mattress on top of a couch was lifted into the air. I scrambled to my feet and rushed into the dining room and then dragged the housekeeper back into the kitchen, where she lay flat on the floor for safety. I thought we were finished. Planks, bricks, and glass blown into the air by the explosion came tumbling down on the house, through the windows and roof, and clouds of smoke and bomb fumes rolled into the rooms. After what seemed an eternity the crashing stopped, and we heard Graebner's voice through the darkness.

GRAEBNER: We decided to go outside and see what had happened. Our massive front door stood wide open, its hinges sprung. The steel frame of the Yale lock had been blown clean off the door jamb. We stepped onto the porch, and across the steps we saw a twisted mass of wreckage. We played our torches on it and then all chorused, "It's a plane!" Sure enough, it was a hunk of the body of a Junkers bomber, about the size of a coffin. It looked like the wreck of an automobile after being hit by a locomotive, and every few inches it was pock-marked by fist-size ack ack holes. A woman screamed from somewhere in the garden in the middle of the square, and Michie dashed across the street to help her while the housekeeper and I ducked inside our doorway to dodge the shrapnel that was raining down. The housekeeper was very worried and kept shouting, "Mr. Michie, come back inside. Think of your wife and baby in America."

MICHIE: The street was littered with debris and ankle deep with glass, but I managed to stumble across into the garden, where I found a dazed woman, unable to find her way to the public shelter in the middle of the square. She sobbed that she had just escaped from the corner house, three doors away from us, in which the German plane had crashed. One of its bombs had exploded as it sailed across the square, and, we learned later, a land mine had gone off when it fell into the house. I must have been somewhat dazed myself, for instead of leading her to the public shelter, I guided her across the street toward her demolished house. By this time her house and the ones next door and several others across the street were blazing fiercely. I realized what I was doing just in time and turned about and started back for the public shelter. At the garden gate I found two other women huddling, with blankets over their nightgowns, and led all three down the path to the shelter entrance. Then I ran for the house. When I saw the plane wreckage on the steps I determined that we had to have a souvenir for the evening's ordeal, so Graebner and I carefully carried Goering's little gift into our hall.

GRAEBNER: After a few minutes we reassembled in the cellar and, over three stiff shots of neat Scotch, discussed our next move. We quickly agreed that the combined danger of more bombs being dropped round the flaming target, unexploded time bombs which might be in the plane wreckage, and the possibility that our own house might go up in flames made it imperative to leave home at once. We didn't stop to collect any belongings, and Michie and I reluctantly agreed that we'd best leave my dog, who'd been shut in the kitchen after the second explosion, behind in the house. But our housekeeper begged us to take him, so we made a last dash upstairs for him. We had gone only a few feet into the street when we saw that it was so full of splintered glass and debris that he had to be carried.

MICHIE: We stumbled along the streets in the direction of a railroad station, where we hoped to find a taxi. By the light of the fires we could see pitiful groups of people running from their basement shelters to the undamaged public shelter in the square. Others stood helplessly in their doorways, not knowing whether to risk running through the streets or stay in their threatened homes. Halfway to the station another bright-red glow suddenly lit up the street around the corner from us. I knew what was coming from experience. Just as the explosion came, we threw ourselves into the doorway of a concrete building. The bomb made a direct hit on a building two doors away, but fortunately around the corner, so the blast didn't touch us. We hurried on, and in front of the station found a solitary cab, the driver of which was willing to risk a run to the Dorchester Hotel. We could have kissed him.

GRAEBNER: The lobby was thick with socialites and diplomats, with great and near-great Londoners, who eyed us as if we were refugees from a concentration camp. Even my old friend Richmond Temple, the Dorchester's publicity chief, failed to recognize me through my coating of grime, but when I explained what had happened to us he beamed, "The hotel is yours. Nothing is too good for the first Americans to bring down a German plane." We didn't think we were that good, but, after packing the housekeeper off to bed, Michie and I took him at his word. We celebrated before we went to bed with the familiar symphony of the ack ack guns blasting away overhead. Earlier, as we were sitting at the bar, my hand suddenly went to my pocket in a sort of post-hypnotic gesture and pulled out a teacup. I don't remember putting it there, but I must have picked it up before leaving the shelter.

MICHIE: In the morning we discovered that our housekeeper had taken a taxi to the house at five o'clock, before the all-clear had sounded. The square and streets around were roped off because of the presence of delayed-action bombs, but she badgered her way past police and A.R.P. men and made five trips upstairs to salvage a couple of suits, shirts, and toilet articles for us. It wasn't until she'd finished her salvage job that she realized the risk she took: one big delayed-action bomb was buried in our back garden, four more were planted in adjoining gardens, and two were buried in the vegetable garden, which A.R.P. wardens had carefully cultivated atop the public shelter in the square.

"Up Periscope!"

by

AN OFFICER OF H.M. SUBMARINE *STURGEON*

VIII. "UP PERISCOPE!"

ON THE evening of September 2, the small British submarine *Sturgeon*, 740 tons, commanded by Lieutenant George David Archibald Gregory, was on patrol on the *inside* of a German mine field off the north coast of Denmark. There it intercepted and sunk a 10,000-ton German transport which was traveling toward Norway with four thousand German troops, guns, and ammunition. It is believed that most of these soldiers perished, for many hundreds of bodies were later washed up on the coast of Norway.

The troopship had an escort of destroyers and aircraft. There was half a gale blowing at the time, it was nearly dark, and the submarine was in a bad position to attack when the convoy was first sighted. But Lieutenant Gregory stalked the ship for some time, and by extraordinarily good marksmanship (which he describes as "luck") he managed to strike home with his torpedoes from a distance of over two miles. Gregory had previously received the D.S.O. for submarine work on "hazardous duties."

Gregory is thirty, married, with one child. He is a Scot,

son of a gunner colonel, and has been in the Submarine Service for nine years. He thinks it is "the best game there is."

This is the story of the *Sturgeon:* When we slid out into the North Sea from our home base on that late August afternoon, I had no idea of the amazing piece of luck which awaited us. For, contrary to general belief, we in "The Trade" [Navy's name for the Submarine Service] get precious little real excitement as a rule and hardly a target to shoot at from one month's end to another. Whereas a U-boat captain has only to poke his nose out of his home waters to find the sea stiff with targets, we usually find "enemy waters" empty from the beginning of our patrol to the end of it. No fat convoys, no crowded troopships, no enemy warships stripped for action and looking for trouble.

For most of us our patrols have meant long weeks of boredom and routine. We hunt in a void which seldom offers a chance of action to alleviate the monotony. By day we comb the endless sea miles of our assigned "beat," traveling just under periscope depth and popping up every few minutes to have a look round. It's "Up periscope. . . . Down periscope" all the hours of daylight.

At night we rest on the surface to recharge the batteries. The off-duty men come along then to stand in little groups smoking and gossiping under the open hatch of the conning tower. This is the time, too, for "hot cooking," because the fresh night air drives away the stale air and the all-pervading stink of Diesel oil from the engines.

As usual, the first few days of this trip were quiet. When we reached the outer fringe of our patrol area—a spot well within enemy waters—the weather was steadily getting worse, but we saw nothing. Then we began to inch our way through what the Germans had declared to be a mine field. Eventually we reached waters which we judged would be a very good place to intercept anything coming from the German eastern ports. Patrolling up and down, we saw nothing the first few days except one or two aircraft, which didn't worry us very much because the sea was too rough for them to spot the faint feathering of our periscope. It is in calm weather that we have to be careful of aircraft, for then they can see not only the periscope feather but our shadow below the surface of the water.

On the fifth day of our patrol, just as it was getting dark, I noticed one aircraft in the distance which seemed to be taking a lot of interest in the sea beneath. It kept buzzing around within a three-mile radius. I was feeling pretty annoyed that we had seen nothing so far, and this aircraft was a bit of a nuisance, because we wanted to keep at periscope depth for the last of the daylight. Handing over to his No. 1 [first lieutenant], the captain went along to our little wardroom to check over some reports.

He had hardly sat down when the No. 1 reported that the

two men at the hydrophones had picked up the faint, far-off beat of ship's engines. He jumped up and raced into the control room. The hydrophone men had got a bearing on those distant engines. They reported the sound of several ships. "To hell with that aircraft," I thought. "We're coming up to have a jolly good look round." Sure enough came the order "Up periscope."

Through the eyepiece I first saw only the green translucent wash of the sea, but then, as the glass cleared the surface waves, I spotted a German destroyer silhouetted against the after glare of the dying sun. Seven-eighths of the horizon was dark, but there in the one clear patch was the enemy ship. The order "Diving stations" was given.

The captain watched the destroyer for a minute or two and then passed another order to the coxswain, perched unemotionally at the hydroplane wheel, to bring her up a few feet. I had another quick glance as the captain passed the eyepiece to me. Droplets of sea water flew down across the crystal-bright surface of the lens as I swung the periscope round a bit. And there, just behind the first destroyer, another ship loomed up! This was a large, handsome transport. Behind was another small destroyer. They were about three miles off to the northwest of me, clearly heading toward Oslo.

This was a tremendous moment for us. Here was the thing we had been waiting for during all these wearisome patrols. And it was big game, too.

But the captain had to think fast. The light was going, and we were in about the worst possible position to attack. The enemy ships were just ahead of us on our beam and steaming a parallel course, but in the opposite direction. We had to alter course quickly and travel unseen to a position from which, on a converging track, our torpedoes would have the maximum chance of striking home. I remember the captain taking his eye away from the lens for a moment and seeing the No. 1 and the men in the control room watching him eagerly. "A big one," he said to them briefly, "with a destroyer escort."

Another look at the swiftly oncoming ships, a glance at the bearing figures on the periscope, a last summing up of our position, and he issued the order, "Blow all torpedo tubes." [Drive water out of tubes and insert torpedoes ready for firing.] He stayed at the lens for another moment, getting a last "fix" and giving the information and orders which would bring us to our next position: "Bearing red seven 0; I am 20 degrees starboard; port wheel five knots. . . . Steer 350 degrees. . . . DOWN PERISCOPE."

The next few minutes, as the boat slowly turned under water to get on to the new course, we worried ourselves sick. Had we estimated the enemy course and speed aright? How long were we going to be getting round? Where would they be when we put the periscope up again?

Impatiently, the captain watched the torpedo tubes' signal lights. I heard him snap out to our No. 1, "When the hell are Nos. 2 and 4 going to be ready?" But before he had even finished the sentence the "readiness" signals flashed up. I watched the silent men at the depth-control valves. The electric driving motors whined louder, flooding into the silence in the control room. Then again he called, "UP PERISCOPE!"

There they were—much nearer, but at a new angle. The Germans had altered course slightly. "We might miss them yet," I thought. So the captain yelled another series of hurried orders, which, with the answers, went something like this:

CAPTAIN (at periscope): Bearing, green 25 degrees.

THIRD HAND (at instrument showing bearing of submarine to target): You are now 25 degrees starboard, sir.

CAPTAIN: Oh, Lord, no! He's more than that. Give him 45 degrees.

THIRD HAND: Enemy's new course then on 40 degrees.

CAPTAIN: DOWN PERISCOPE. Starboard wheel. Nine knots. Steer 310 degrees. Down 50 feet.

COXSWAIN: Fifty feet, sir.

CAPTAIN: Slow both. [Slowing engines so periscope will not feather too much on breaking water.] Periscope depth. UP PERISCOPE!"

The rest was a matter of seconds. We were closing rapidly,

and even at our distance of about two and a half miles and in the last of the light the white water could be seen breaking away from the speeding transport's bow. She was dead on our line of sight. "Stand by!" ordered the captain without taking his eye away from the lens. He pressed the button of his stopwatch and counted as the angle was closing. "One . . . two . . . three." Then: "FIRE!" The rating who had been standing by the firing panel, head cocked expectantly toward him, pushed home the switches.

I felt the boat shudder as the torpedoes left her and sped on their way. I had a last look. The transport, curiously it seemed to me, was steaming serenely on against that patch of light to the northwest. Then the captain bellowed, "DOWN PERISCOPE." . . . "Down 60 feet." We waited in dead silence, our eyes fixed on the minute hand of the control-room clock. It seemed to creep round the dial. One minute went by, then two, and my doubts and uncertainties began to grow agonizing. I strained my ears for a distant sound, but heard only the hum and ticktock of the giro near the helmsman, the faint noises of the sea outside the hull, and the glug-glug of the ballast tanks as we kept our depth. "We've missed," I thought gloomily. "We've missed her." We would not have another chance. We could not attack again at the altered angle.

In that instant, when I had given up all hope, I heard a

distant muffled bang. Then another and another. All the light bulbs flickered for a moment or two. A gentle tremor shook the deck plates beneath me. The captain from his swivel seat near the instrument panels sprang up and ordered the submarine to periscope depth. He had a quick look and then silently handed the glass to me. I thought first that the coating of sea spume would never clear from the glass, but then in a flash the whole terrific picture leaped into view. An enormous column of black smoke reared high above the transport. To the left and right of it, giant fireballs, which must have been exploding ammunition, arched outward against the background of darkening sky. The captain turned to the men in the control room, who were staring at him questioningly. "She's gone," he said. Their faces broke into broad grins. One of the ratings slid out of the control room to take the "buzz" [news] along to the men forward. He watched that distant scene for a moment more and then, just as I had replaced him at the eyepiece, I suddenly spotted the escort aircraft making a beeline back along our torpedo tracks toward us. These tracks must still have been faintly visible, for less than three minutes had passed since that first distant bang. Down we shot once more.

For the next few minutes we waited anxiously, wondering if the aircraft had seen us and had called up the destroyers. Any moment we expected the thud and shake of the depth charges. At the captain's hand signal the men in the control room froze into stillness. Those at hydrophones bent over their gear listening hard. The first few minutes were awful. But nothing happened, so he decided to come up and have another look.

It was now completely dark, and I saw the transport was on fire from stem to stern. The reflection from the flames seemed to make a patch across the waters toward me. And against the vast red glow I could pick out the silhouettes of the destroyers passing and repassing. I watched the flaming ship for a long time as we cruised gently along at periscope depth. After an hour, when we saw that she was obviously a goner, the captain gave the order to dive down deep and reload torpedo tubes.

We stayed down about an hour, still hearing nothing except the very distant sound of ship's engines. As it was getting rather late and the air was thickening, we decided to surface cautiously. Unfortunately we came up "beam on" to the target position. I was first onto the bridge through the conning-tower hatch, and as I got there we were suddenly lit up from end to end in the blinding glare of a searchlight. That moment was perhaps the worst of the whole episode. I stood absolutely glued to the bridge rail for a second or two. Then the searchlight moved on. They hadn't seen us! The searchlights were obviously combing the sea for survivors, and after a while they began to dim. The destroyers were moving away from us.

I stayed on the bridge while the watch was posted and filled my lungs with the good fresh air. Suddenly I felt more tired than I have ever been in my life. On the distant dark horizon there was an occasional flicker of signal and recognition lights from enemy vessels, which had no doubt come out to meet the escort destroyers. But there was no sound except the noise of the rising gale and the breaking seas. We cruised slowly on, recharging our batteries. The normal routine of the boat started again. Up through the conning-tower hatch I could catch the smell of bacon and eggs frying for breakfast. It was quiet again and all the tension was over. There was one minor tragedy, however, before that night was over. The rating ordered up to polish the great object glass of the periscope reported that there was no petrol left in the small bottle, which is all we are allowed to carry in submarines. It is essential that this glass should take the highest possible polish so that water droplets will not adhere to the surface and spoil periscope vision. There was nothing to do but hand over the last two inches that remained in my only bottle of fine old brandy. That was a terrible blow. But I watched that rating like a lynx to see that all the brandy went on the polishing cloth and not down his throat.

Our House Was Bombed

by

MRS. LILIAN MARGARET HART

IX. OUR HOUSE WAS BOMBED

THE crudest, most cruel, and least effective attacks of the Nazi Luftwaffe have been its indiscriminate bombing of the homes and properties of the people of Britain. With the open attacks on British cities—particularly the raids on London, which began on a large scale in August, 1940,—the catchphrase "the citizens are in the front line of modern war" lost its metaphorical sense and became a reality.

The narrator of this story, thirty-nine-year-old Mrs. Lilian Margaret Hart, was singled out for no act of heroism. Her spirit was no higher, her sufferings no greater than those of hundreds of thousands of housewives in Britain's civilian army. But she—and the story she tells—is typical of those who stand beside her in the front line.

Mrs. Hart and her husband, thirty-six-year-old Henry George Hart, lived in the grubby working-class East End district of London's Bethnal Green Road. For six months before the war, Mr. Hart took government courses in A.R.P. work, first-aid, and anti-gas training. When the war started, he became one of the nation's 200,000 full-time A.R.P. wardens, paid $16 per week. His post during raids was just outside the Church of St. James the Great on Bethnal Green Road. Their home was directly behind the church, over the church clubrooms, which Mrs. Hart cleaned and looked after.

This is Mrs. Hart's story: Our house doesn't look like much now! Just a dirty heap for the dustman to cart away. You'd never think four rooms and a bathroom could change so much, all in just half a minute.

George—his proper name is Henry George Hart, but he never uses the Henry—was on duty at the warden's post, and I had just been in to evening service at the church, our own church here, St. James the Great. I've belonged here for eighteen years, and Sunday was the National Day of Prayer. When I got home I changed into my old skirt and jumper and called to Gyp, our dog. We were going down to the corner to meet George, like we always do. He works a twelve-hour shift, and was due home at 8 P.M.

I know it was a little past eight, because I heard the clock strike in the tower and I was wondering what was keeping George. Then the warning went. I hurried back to the house, because, though I'm not a warden or anything, somebody needs to show the neighbors the way to the shelter under the vicarage. It's the strongest house around here. None of the people have their own shelters, because their yards are too small.

The siren hadn't hardly ended when I heard a screamer coming down. I hurried the last people into the shelter—or what I thought was the last. Then I sent Gyp and his friend Bob, the black dog, upstairs to my kitchen. They always crawl under the scullery table during a raid.

After that I had another last look around. I flashed my torch through the shelter passage and then heard two ladies coming through. I got them down and into the stockhold— not the proper shelter, but it's underground where the church furnace is. I noticed three of our club boys sitting in the little clubroom beside the passage here, playing solo, and I told them they'd better get down, but they said no.

I'd just left them and was crossing the yard here when I heard it. Terrible loud, it sounded, and coming awful close. I just opened the vicarage door and stood tight, hanging onto the door with my hands. I remember thinking it would be better to have the door open than to have the glass blown over me.

It seemed like nearly a minute between the thud when it fell and the roar of the explosion. It was dusky by that time and black inside the hallway, so I couldn't see anything, but afterward for a minute or two I could hear crowds and crowds of glass and wood coming down all around. It's a miracle I wasn't hit, standing there.

Then somebody in the hallway shouted, "Get 'em out. Get 'em out." And somebody else shouted, "Fire." And somebody else shouted, "Keep 'em in," and a woman in the shelter was moaning, and all the kids were crying.

I knew it wasn't fire. I would have seen it by that time. But I went out to the front exit of the shelter, in Bethnal Green Road, and helped some of them out, and some of them went across the street to another shelter. But most of them stayed. We was all choking with the soot and dust, and there was a burnt taste of gunpowder in my mouth.

Then I went out in the back again, and it was then for the first time that I can remember I saw there wasn't anything where my bedroom had been. It's funny, but really I didn't feel a thing. I remember somebody asked me, "Do you feel all right?" I guess they were expecting me to conk out. But I remember just looking up there where the house used to be and then sort of not thinking about it any more. You know how you'll do when you've lost something, or misplaced it. And you just think to yourself you'll hunt for it later on, but you don't waste time worrying about it at the time.

What I was worrying about was George and my cat Timmy. I kept calling and calling for him—Timmy—Timmy—but I couldn't hear a sound. I think he died quick like—didn't know what hit him, I hope. And the dogs, too. They found Gyp today, way up on the roof of the vestry, and the black dog was just hanging over a broken rafter there. I hope they died quick, too.

Then somebody told me George was all right. He'd been on duty at his post right out in front of the vicarage, and he'd dived behind his little pile of sandbags when it hit. He counted slowly to four, like the wardens are supposed to, to avoid the falling bits before they stand up. He knew it was his own sector because the explosion was so loud. Then he went into the vicarage to telephone the control center at the town hall. Once he'd done that, he told me later, he got a weakening at the knees. He was always a man for his home, you know, fond of it and all, and always pottering about. A couple of wardens held him up and walked him about a bit until he felt better. I didn't see him till much later, though.

I stayed on working and helping in the shelter till five o'clock in the morning. We didn't do tea that night because we'd run short. They used to allow us a pound and a half for shelter use, and we sold it at a penny a cup and gave the money to the church for extra lighting and gas. But even without the tea there was plenty to do.

I went back to the shelter. Two or three people had fainted. That's only natural, really, with a bomb so close. So I went about with the sal volatile. If you've got money, you can afford whiskey instead of sal volatile. But it does the business just as well. I dabbed a little lavender water on a handkerchief and wiped the women's foreheads, or gave them smelling salts. I got some jugs of water and dished them out. There were other bombs falling around all the time—we could hear them. So it wasn't really safe to leave the shelter. And I'd had to see some of the women to the w.c. up the stairs; and some of the kiddies were sick, so I washed up after them. Somebody's got to do it. In the end I took a pail down for the little kiddies to use.

When it got daylight and the all-clear came, Mr. Lester—he's a warden in George's post—asked us to go to his house. His wife's evacuated. So we went over and had tea and a wash. We were in a filthy state. Like a couple of sweeps, we were. Then I came back, just to look around at the house. You never know who might be around to pick things up, and we had a little money saved in a tin box. I was hoping to find that. I didn't, but one of the boys did later and handed it over to us.

When we went back at seven-thirty in the morning to look around I heard that the three boys that were playing cards in the little clubroom when the bomb fell had been hit and bruised, and that one of them got a piece of wood between his shoulder blades. I never knew it until later, but I found that, after I'd had my last look around before the bomb, three other women came in the passage. They got it awful bad, and were rushed right off to hospital.

Then I caught a train for Dagenham to tell Mum— George's mother. I was afraid she might hear it from somebody else and be worried. I told her we've none of us got a home now. But we should be glad we've got our health. I mean that's all we've got—and George's job. I'm glad Mum was out of it, though. We only sent her away on Saturday. If she'd been here, we both would have been gone, she and me. Being old, she takes a while to get down the stairs, and I would have been with her.

Later on I hunted for Timmy again. I thought there might be just a chance he was still alive. I found Mum's bed thrown right over the church hall, and her black pleated skirt hanging all slashed and torn from a bush on the other side of the vicarage. I found my ration cards, too, and a pair of George's pajamas he'd just bought, still in the cellophane paper, but the paper was slit all up and down like somebody had cut it with a scissors.

I picked up a little china jug absolutely uncracked in our ruins, but it wasn't mine. Somebody from the pub on the corner had put it there for a joke. You know how you're always reading in the paper about a house being bombed but a bowl of eggs in the pantry not even being cracked. I say it couldn't be. In our house there's not one stick of furniture unbroken, and you couldn't get solider stuff.

George was a cabinetmaker, ever since he was fourteen, and he himself made everything we had in the house—tables and the chests of drawers and our bed and the china bureau. Every bit of it out of solid mahogany, and made by hand— all but the piano. It took him a long time to do it after we was married. Oh, it was a beautiful house we had—not that you could tell now.

The demolition squad found some drawers still in one piece, and George's winter woolies, socks, and jumpers and things are in them, still all right but filthy dirty. But I can't find my blankets. I'd had 'em cleaned ready for winter, all nice and neat in the linen chest. A pair of my blue silk knickers is still on the roof of the vestry, and some of my curtains too. Eee! And I saw a piece of my kitchen curtains sticking to Mrs. Warren's wall across the street. Somebody found my ring case. Fancy, a little thing like that, with both my rings, my diamond and my wedding ring in it still! I take them off when I'm cleaning up around. And they dug out my vacuum cleaner, still in its box. I wish they'd find Mum's bag. It's got her pension book in it. And my housekeeping money and my wages and some odd bits of church club money, £3 or £4 in all, are knocking about somewhere.

It's awful lucky getting the biscuit tin back and unbroken.

It had all our savings in it. We've been careful, you know. With our money saved, we can manage better than a lot of people around here. We had £20 saved, and our insurance books in it, and eight war bonds that cost fifteen shillings each. We've got a fire-insurance policy too, but I don't fancy we can get anything on it now. We just recently took out a policy for air raids, too. It's crazy the things we've found. A box of my husband's handkerchiefs, and another box with mine in it. A cooking spoon, the middle flap of my dining table, and a cut-glass vase without a crack in it—but it's not one of my best ones, the wedding-present ones.

We'll never be able to replace our wedding presents. We were married here in the church on December 23, 1933. George used to sing in the choir here, but I met him at another church club, St. Jude's, down the road. We were both born in Bethnal Green and lived here all our lives, so you can imagine the wedding presents we had. A lovely canteen of cutlery, and some beautiful cut-glass, and linen and all.

Everybody around has been awful kind to us. My sister-in-law's sister lent me a dress. Somebody else gave me bloomers and a vest, and an old lady came along with a parcel for what she calls the "refugees." Another friend of mine sent me ten shillings. Poor little devil, she can't afford it. Her husband's a soldier.

I don't think I want to come back to Bethnal Green Road

to live. I want to get a job. I don't think it's a good thing to sit and think—it just makes it seem worse. George says we won't try to set up a proper home—at least not till the war's over. He hasn't got the time now to build furniture, and I don't think he's got the heart, not right now anyway. And me, I wouldn't be bothered to make curtains again and do crochet and fix everything nice again. Not now.

Fire over London

by

AUXILIARY FIREMAN LOUIS A. WILSON

X. FIRE OVER LONDON

O N THE afternoon of Saturday, September 7, 1940, the Germans launched their first great daylight raid against London, concentrating on a section of the docks. High-explosive bombs, followed by incendiaries, were dropped, the purpose being to start a great chain of fires to serve as beacons for the night bombers which would follow.

The tactics succeeded. When dusk fell, fires started in dockland could be seen thirty miles away. On that day and night the 30,000 men of London's Auxiliary Fire Service, in co-operation with regular units of the Brigade, went into action on a large scale for the first time. They were bombed unceasingly while fighting the fires. But had it not been for their heroic and tremendous efforts, the consequences for London might have been much more serious than they were.

This is the story of one of them. He is Louis Abbott ("Tug") Wilson, a section officer of the A.F.S., who is in control of a squad of six men. He is thirty-seven, married, and has two boys. Before the war he was a motor mechanic, but ever since he could walk and talk, he says, his ambition has been to be a fireman.

This is Tug's story: I was talking cricket to the sub-station officer when the "shout"—our name for the fire alarm—came through on the phone. The order was to take every available appliance to Pageant Wharf, a fire station in the heart of dockland. The W.A.F.S. [Women's Auxiliary Fire Service] clerk on duty in the office jumped to the alarm cord, bells clanged throughout the building, and we were off.

It was about five-thirty on that Saturday afternoon, and we had been standing by ever since the air-raid sirens had wailed out the first warning about midday. All that time there had been the steady roll of A.A. gunfire and the thud of bombs toward the east. And as we swung out into the bright sunshine, I knew we were in for something pretty serious, for whole streams of the great red appliances of the regular London Fire Brigade were thundering past us, their bells hammering, and the handholds packed with clinging men. They were going in the same direction, but they came from stations even farther from the fire than ours.

We raced on, going hell for leather in one great, clanging company. Passing gray old Lambeth Palace, London residence of the Archbishop of Canterbury, to reach the main roads running east, I had time to reflect that this old place, which had seen the Great Fire of London and many other things in its time, had never seen a turnout like this. Looking up between two of its Tudor towers, I saw ten Dorniers wheeling and glinting near a cloud patch, with our fighters weaving in among them. They were going south, and had probably done their job; or, I thought hopefully, they had not been able to break through to the docks area. I could see bombs falling well away in the southern suburbs.

By now we were in the Old Kent Road. We were having a fairly clear run, because most of the busses and the motor traffic along that usually crowded street had pulled into the curb and emptied their passengers into shelters. At the lower end, however, we ran into the first wreckage—shops and houses demolished by German bombs which had missed the docks. Once or twice we skirted bomb craters crazily on two wheels, with the pump trailer slewing wildly at all angles. We hung on like grim death as we bounced over the wreckage and around corners. And over the clanging of our fire-bells and the roar of our engine, I could hear the unceasing thud of explosions ahead and coming nearer.

I don't remember feeling anything much about it except a sort of tenseness. I had enough to do holding on and keeping an eye on the way to do much thinking. But I do remember half wondering how we would get down to it, now that it had come to the real thing.

We were a mixed squad, but typical enough of the A.F.S. In my section I had an ex-insurance salesman, a meat porter from Smithfield Meat Market, a South African who had come to Europe for a good time and joined the A.F.S. when he had gambled all his money away. The others were a Maltese-born bank teller, a printer, a perfume packer, and a concrete worker. The biggest jobs we had ever turned out for during our year of training and waiting just for this had been an occasional chimney fire and a smoke-filled boarding-house where a sleepy lodger had set his bedclothes alight with a cigarette.

A lot of people regarded us as a joke, as something like the Keystone comedy fire brigades of the early films. They used to gather round at our outdoor practice sessions, ready for a good laugh. More Londoners used to grumble that the whole twenty thousand of us were an expensive liability who got £3 a week and keep just for riding around in our taxicab trailers and polishing a bit of brasswork.

But now, down in that wrecked section of working-class homes near the docks, there were little knots of people at every street corner, who stood there, bombs or no bombs, cheering us on and pointing the way. As we went clanging past the corners, they grinned and waved, shouting directions and good-humored cracks after us: "Second to the left, cock, and keep goin'!" "Got your asbestos suits with you?" Sometimes there were warning shouts: "Miss the third turning; that street's bombed." They were cheerful and grand in all that hellish racket and ruin, and I just felt warm and proud. We'd do anything for those people. Just show us to it.

Hurtling round one corner, we rolled over the pavement to miss a bomb crater. Our two rear tires, pierced with window glass which littered the pavement, suddenly blew out with a bang. The firetruck lurched into the air and flung some of us off into the road. As I picked myself up, I could see round the bend toward the river a solid wall of smoke and fire stretching, it seemed, for miles. Other appliances, luckier than us, were flying past us on the way. Furious at this mishap within sight of our goal, we piled into the job of replacing the damaged tires. In the middle of the change job, a Bren gun-carrier, manned by a Canadian crew on the way into London, pulled up alongside. The crew jumped off and lent a hand. I think we beat all world's records on or off a motor race track in changing those wheels. In only a minute or two we were off again, going full out.

At the Pageant Wharf station they ordered us off to Gate L of the Surrey Commercial Docks to tackle a fire at a certain wharf. We drove off through the deserted streets which ran along the dock walls. They were littered with the debris of houses, and opposite the gate a block of workmen's flats was blazing, set on fire by the sparks and heat from over the dock walls.

As we turned in at Gate L, a spectacle which I shall never forget to my dying day lay before us. From end to end the dockside was aflame. The water itself seemed alight. But that came from burning barges. Across the water an island jetty was blazing, and from left, right, and all around, the heat waves struck us in the face like a blow. I felt numb. So did the others, they admitted afterward, but we went through all the proper motions.

I saw that most of the burning stuff was timber which had been stacked along the dockside. It had been set alight by sparks from loaded barges on which, presumably, the bombs had fallen. On each side I could see huge walls of what we call "hot smoke"—thick, black stuff shot through with billowing gusts of flame. I could only hope that the thickening clouds through which we were passing would not turn into "hot smoke." But we had to chance it to get our suction down into the water from the quayside.

When we reached the quay, I found, on my left, a very big warehouse which was not yet touched. But the danger spot was those blazing barges, from which the wind was carrying flame and sparks. Even the surface of timber rafts lying between the barges and the quay, wood which had been soaking in the water for many months, was now alight. I imme-

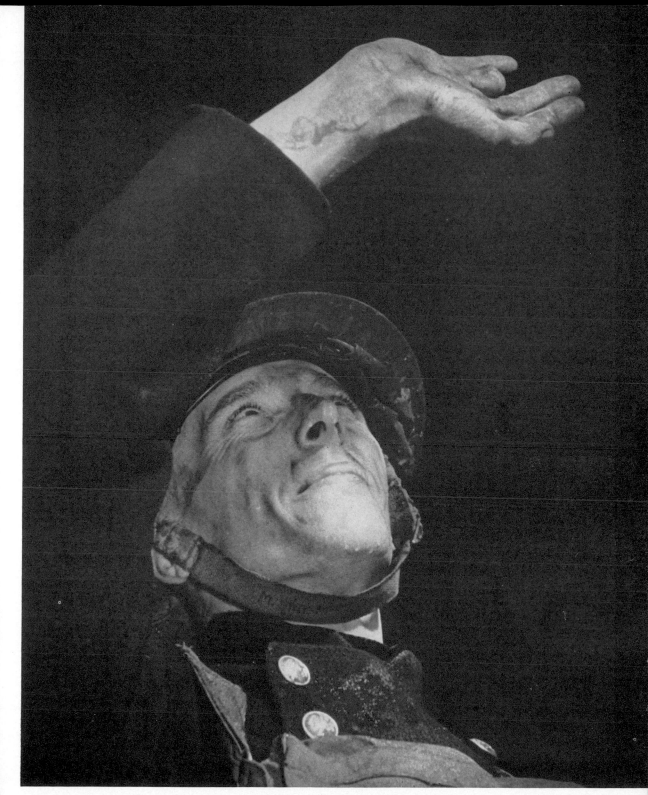

FIRE OVER LONDON

AUXILIARY FIREMAN LOUIS A. (TUG) WILSON

FIRE OVER LONDON

FLAMES BY DAY

FIRE OVER LONDON

FLAMES BY NIGHT

NIGHT ALARM

TROOP SERGEANT MAJOR STEPHEN H. BAKER

NIGHT ALARM

A.A. BATTERY IN ACTION AT NIGHT

FRONT-LINE GIRL

SONIA VERA CARLYLE STRAW, G.M.

FRONT-LINE GIRL

A DOG IS RESCUED

HAWKER HURRICANE CLIMBING FAST

I FOUGHT OVER LONDON

AERIAL COMBAT

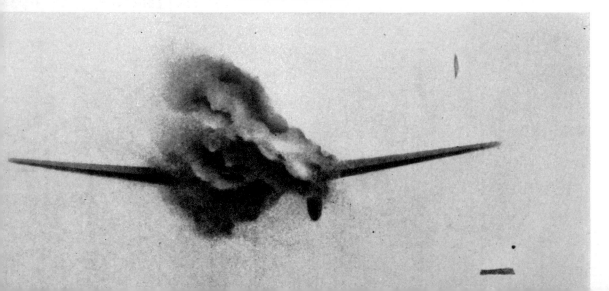

diately saw that the only way to save the shed and to fight the fire to left and right of us was to sink those barges.

So we got the suction down, played the hoses on the timber rafts, then ran out several branches of hose across the rafts, and began to pour water into the barges in the hope of sinking them. Other branches were run out to keep the shed watered down and to play to right and left of us so as to preserve a way of escape.

The first few hours seem like a nightmare to me now. I knew that night had fallen, but only by my watch and the sky, which had vanished from sight above the crest of the flames. I remember odd snatches of things: Eddie Donlevy, the ex-porter from Smithfield, and his masterly understatement as we drove through the gates into that inferno and looked around at our first job. "Well," he said, "this *is* a bit of a bastard!"

Eddie was the newest member of my squad—he didn't even have a full uniform—but he gave a standout performance. Once I saw him, in a muffler, dungarees, and tin hat, silhouetted against the flames as he stood far out on the rafts and tossed blazing planks into the water. Another time he flung himself head first on a hose branch which had broken loose and was flailing crazily about. He is a pretty strong boy, and you have to be to hold down a hose branch which has 100 lb. pressure to the square inch on it. If the nozzle end hits the men, it can break their legs. The orthodox way of handling a loose branch is to signal the engineman to shut off pressure, but this wasn't possible that night. Eddie kept our spirits up with his wisecracks. Later, when we suddenly became aware that more bombs were tumbling down around the blazing target, it was Eddie who cracked, "Blimey, if it hasn't bloody well started raining again."

I can remember some moments when I felt pretty black. Once, coming back from the gates with some fresh water to drink and to steep the handkerchiefs which we tied across our faces against the colossal heat, I saw our hoses disappearing into the smoke and flame where we were working. I suddenly felt that we were cut off and alone. Again, emerging on to the quayside and looking at the gigantic blaze all around, I thought, "How bloody hopeless—all London's alight." But then, when I looked across to the island which had previously been all flame and saw smoke and steam coming up, I felt cheered up again and thought, "They're fighting it there, anyhow. And we'll beat it yet." The sight of two more of these damned barges sinking at last was cheering, but that lonely feeling, cut off there in that sea of flames, persisted. You see, we had seen nobody and had no news of any kind for some hours, and we did not know how far the new German attack had developed. About 9:30 P.M., however, the District Superintendent came walking toward us through an avenue of smoke and flame. God knows how he had found us in this obscure corner of what was beginning to look like a suburb of hell.

He is a gray-haired old-time regular, and was fighting fires before I was born. His eyes are screwed up from the smoke of some of those forgotten fires. In the service they call him "The Salamander."

After I had shown him round our little spot and explained my trick with the barges, he nodded briefly and said, "Good work." I couldn't have felt better if the King himself had congratulated me. He took me along the quayside and pointed out a place which had been hidden from our view, and said that another unit was having a bad time there. We could see them dimly in the glare playing their hoses away from the dockside, and they seemed almost cut off. He told me to watch out in case I got a signal from them, in which event we were to run hoses round and cut through to help them out. He had no other news except all the trouble was around our area only, and we were holding it. Then he stalked off again into the smoke.

I watched that unit for a while. They gave no signal, but suddenly I saw them pushing their trailer appliance over the dockside into the water. From that I judged that it was all up, but there was still a way out on foot for the crews. They did not want to call on me, and dumping the appliance into the dock would at least save it from the flames. It could be dredged up afterward.

I made my way back to my own unit, and it was then that the worst part of the night started. The first explosion about a hundred yards away blew me over on my back and sent flaming hunks of timber soaring skyward. It was really a terrifying sight.

"What the hell was that?" I shouted to the pump man. "Gas main gone up?" "No," he yelled back. "Raid. Been on some time." For a second or two the mere thought of us standing nakedly on the edge of a clearly lit target gave me that real sinking feeling. Then there was another, and another crash near by. There was no time to think. We flung ourselves down, nuzzling into the wet ashes and mud, but still holding onto the hose branches. One bomb hit the end of the raft in the dock and blew out great lumps of two-foot-square timber. A huge column of water came over the dock wall and nearly drowned us—as if we were not wet enough already. Looking up for a split-second, I saw a thirty-foot length of heavy timber from a raft turning slowly over and over in mid-air above the dock. Just then I heard Eddie Donlevy's remark about it starting to rain again. We hugged the wet earth and laughed.

It seems strange now, but my first clear impression about the bombing was a sort of flabbergasted surprise. In the work of fighting that fire I had forgotten all about raids and everything else. We had been working in such a colossal racket from the crackling of burning timber and the tremendous din of our fire pumps that it was quite impossible to hear the sound of sirens, aircraft engines, or gunfire. The glare from the fire blanketed the searchlights, so there was nothing to warn us. The bombs were the first intimation that all of us had that the dockland blaze was an easy mark for Jerry.

Something had to be done about it quickly, because more bombs would be coming down when the next relay arrived. But we still had to carry on. We couldn't leave the fire, so I posted a man away from the noise of the pumps. When he heard the whistling air rush of bombs coming down, he was to wave his arms and we would all fling ourselves down.

It worked all right. But we were up and down a good many times that night, and as the hours went on it got a bit wearing. It's not pleasant to be bombed while you are standing in the open and a clear mark among flames, but the men stuck it wonderfully. Gradually we were getting the fire under control. The barges had all been sunk, we had cleared the dockside, and started to work into the burning timber stacks on both sides of us.

Toward 2 A.M. the Superintendent came along again. All the fires in our sector were out by then, so he ordered us along to another to help in cooling down red-hot stacks of timber which were still acting as a beacon for the raiders. That done, he ordered us out into the streets beyond the dock walls to deal with the flares from broken gas mains alongside the gutted workmen's flats. They were a bigger beacon still, and bombs were dropping heavily.

On the way out we passed a shelter with its doors closed. We smashed them open, thinking that there might be people still in there. The electric lights were still on, and there were blankets and clothes about, even a baby's freshly made food still in its dish, but the shelter was empty. The police must have got them out before the flames swept over from the docks and set the flats alight.

I posted the lookout man up the street as we began to deal with the gas blaze and picked a crater I could drop into if he waved when a bomb whistled. I must have been pretty befuddled. I remember picking up half of a brick and carefully placing it on the edge of the crater. Maybe I thought that this bit of brick might help to protect my head from blast if I had to pitch into the hole.

There were others besides firefighters in that world of flame and smoke. Going through the dock gates to the canteen for a welcome cup of tea, I saw a man leaning up against the wall, hands in pockets. What he was doing there, God knows. He was dressed in the cap and choker of a dock laborer. As I passed him he turned nonchalantly and said, "Bit warm in there, isn't it, mate?"

Later that night, as I went off to get some more fresh water, I bumped against another little civilian in that hell from which all others had fled. He was in his Sunday-best clothes, but drenched to the skin. When I asked him about drinking water, he said, "Come on, I'll show you," and led me through avenues of burning dumps to a shed, where he started to fill my canvas bucket at a pump. I asked him what he was doing there. "Well," he said, "I was just coming back from the pictures with my old woman when this happened. I dumped her in a shelter and came on here to help if I could. I know the docks. I work here." Then, after a pause, he added, "But just look at me best brown shoes."

We got all our fires out by dawn, but by that time Jerry had stopped his bombing. As we drove slowly back to the station, little knots of people were just emerging from the safety of their shelters. I'll never forget their faces as they stared blankly at the heaps of rubble which had been their homes.

Night Alarm

by

TROOP SERGEANT MAJOR STEPHEN H. BAKER

XI. NIGHT ALARM

SOME of the most active gun sites in Britain are those guarding the ports on the Bristol Channel. The narrator of this story, Troop Sergeant Major Stephen Henry Baker, is senior noncommissioned officer of a battery of 3.7- and 4-inch guns stationed near the southwest approaches to the Channel. Like Baker, who worked for a tramway company before the war, all the members of the gun crew are former Territorials.

This is Baker's story: It was 11 P.M. The sky was low and dirty, and the night was as black as the Earl of Hell's riding boots. It was not a night for any Jerry aircraft to be about. After a last visit to the "stand-by" crews in their shack near the gun pits, I strolled back to my bunk, looking forward to the first real night's sleep in more than a week. Jerry has kept us so busy in this part of England that sometimes for days we don't get a chance to take our clothes off. At best we manage to snatch a few minutes during the day for a quick strip and a shower. Even then sometimes an alarm goes, and the men, mother-naked except for their battlebowlers, rush to their guns. We don't have much time to lose, for the maximum limit allowed to reach all A.A. gun sites is thirty seconds after the alarm, and this requires some pretty fast moving, since the nearest living hut is a good hundred yards from the guns.

I had just got one gum boot off when the stand-by buzzer went. In an instant I had it back on and was out of the door racing to the fighting map in the command hut. Here the G.P.O. [gun position officer] was already tracking the changing position of the approaching enemy aircraft on the map. This map is divided into action grids or areas, and, by means of a signal system, we know almost second by second the enemy's exact location. It is my job to be with the G.P.O. from the first warning while this is going on.

Out by the guns the stand-by crew were already operating the height-finder and predictors, and had the guns stripped and ready for action, but we don't turn the full crews out until the enemy is actually breaking into our area.

I stood there in the command hut over the lamp-lit map, watching the G.P.O.'s pencil creeping over it in time with the code mutterings from the telephonist. Although by now I've seen that tracking process scores of times, I still get a thrill out of watching the unknown enemy being shadowed across the map and held, as it were, on a pencil point through-out every stage of his journey from the coast. Sometimes the track wiggles, goes back on itself, or goes right off the map. This time, however, it came straight on toward us. When it touched the edge of the grid enclosing our area, the G.P.O. pressed the button which set off the alarm buzzers in all the men's huts round the site.

Outside, I joined the men rushing toward the guns. As I got to the first gun pit, the four 3.7's were already nosing round toward that quarter of the sky where the searchlights were groping among the clouds—first a few lights and then more, all of them aimed over the dark estuary and port, over which our guns stood guard. It was clearing a bit and big gaps were opening in the clouds. The searchlights danced about, feeling the gaps.

In the silence that always follows the clang of breeches being opened and the click of ammunition being loaded into the feed trays, I heard Mike, the battery sergeant, telling one of the men to get his boots from the stand-by shack. Mike always races out without his boots. Far off, but coming nearer, the undulating drone of Jerry's engines reached my ears. The gun muzzles moved round in unison following the search-lights. The G.P.O. was now in position in his little sandbagged enclosure. I could see his steel-helmeted head above the bags, dimly silhouetted against the lights, which were now a solid pillar on the horizon. Next to him was his black cocker spaniel Gus, who always follows him out to the gun pits when a shoot is on and perches on top of the bags—that is, until the guns poop off. Then he streaks off in the direction of the firing, as if he were going to bring the Jerry bomber back in his mouth. But he never returns for hours. The G.P.O. says he's "not a particularly good gun dog."

Suddenly the lights all fused together in one blinding cone, and the spotter shouted "Plane!" Then came the G.P.O.'s quiet order, "Plane! Lay on target." A second later the instrument men in the pit reported, "Height-finder on target. . . . Predictor on target." The drone grew nearer and louder, and I could see the Jerry, a glinting speck trapped in the lights.

All the time the height-finder was chanting his changing figures, the predictor man was calling out the changing fuse settings as his instrument gave them: "Fuse 2, fuse 3." The gun muzzles moved imperceptibly, and the men reported "section on target" as each changed instruction was carried out. It takes minutes to tell, but it all happened in a few seconds. Then, on the tick of the last report, the G.P.O. ordered "Fire!"

Instantly came the colossal flash of the four 3.7's, which shoot a flame thirty feet, and the huge air blast that hits you at the back of the head and feels like the smack from a heavy glove. I watched the first salvo pinking ruddily against that speck twisting and turning in the lights. Then there was the usual hell of a noise as we began pumping it up. The guns fire so fast that inside the pits you can see everything going on by the light of their flashes.

Then, right in the middle of one salvo, the bomber "jinked." It seemed to stagger, caught by one burst near its port wing. It heeled over and went sweeping and spinning down the arc of the sky toward the hidden estuary. The searchlights held it, seemed to wipe it down the sky as it went down out of sight.

The battery stopped firing, and there was silence again except for the ringing in my ears from the gun blasts. The searchlights flicked out one by one. Round the guns the men were busy closing down. But they were cursing because we were not sure whether we had got the Jerry or not. There had been no smoke or fire from the falling bomber. Later, however, we found that the bomber had actually fallen in the estuary.

In his little control post, the G.P.O. was standing up and stretching. Gus, the cocker, had disappeared, as usual, somewhere into the darkness. The men were still busy cleaning out the guns and collecting empty shell cases from the 3.7's.

I was just turning away when I heard Jerry's engines again, but very low down this time, and from behind the direction in which our guns had been firing. There had been no warning from the command room, but we all heard the plane, and the men stood transfixed in the darkness listening. A few searchlights sprang up in its direction and wavered uncertainly, their shafts cut off by the low clouds. It came nearer and nearer, growing all the time in intensity. He was heading in our direction and coming in very low.

There was a scramble round the guns. Jerry was nearer still now, making a huge, undulating roar. Then there came a long, whistling sound. Then another, and another. I knew what that meant and was down in a split second, nosing the ground of the sandbagged control post. The bombs hit almost at the same moment, less than a hundred yards away from the gun pits. In the flashes, I saw the men frozen into astonished postures at the guns, and then the air was full of whistling, flying fragments and soft thuds as the bits hit the ground.

"Good shooting," I thought. And I remember that even in that fraction of a second I gave full marks to the Jerry that had seen our gun flashes far below in the darkness, pooping off at his pal, and had come down to have a crack at us. But in the same instant there came four colossal crashes right overhead—and again the hum of flying pieces of shrapnel.

The searchlights now were lighting up our gun site like day, dancing about crazily and being reflected back from the clouds. The men were working the guns round after their first paralyzed shock, and we pooped off a salvo in the direction of the sound. But it was all over. He had gone. He was the hottest Jerry and the only really tough guy we had come up against in all these months of action and in more than one hundred shoots. I certainly respected him for nicking in from the darkness and trying to give us a packet. When we sorted ourselves out, we found that nobody had been hurt from all the six bombs—the three percussion which had hit the ground and the four time A.P. [anti-personnel] bombs which had exploded overhead.

We so little expected direct attack like this that the sentry, far off in the darkness, had not bothered to take cover when the first bombs whistled down. Later he told us that the first bomb had "flung a lot of dirt and stones" past him. When daylight came we found that the ground near him was studded with bomb splinters, some almost a foot long.

Front-Line Girl

by

SONIA VERA CARLYLE STRAW, G.M.

XII. FRONT-LINE GIRL

CHUB-CHEEKED, auburn-haired, nineteen-year-old Sonia Straw is in the front line of the Battle of Britain. Five days a week she works as a short-hand typist in a solicitor's office in Croydon. Every evening at six she puts on her steel helmet, hangs her gas mask over her shoulder, and cycles to a concrete dugout in her home in a village of East Surrey, where she does a turn of duty until midnight as an Air Raid Precautions warden.

Although she looks no more than a shy little schoolgirl, Sonia has already won her award for bravery under fire in this civilian's war. She was one of the first three women in Britain entitled to sign the initials G.M. after her name. G.M. stands for the George Medal, specially created by King George VI for the recognition of civilian gallantry. It was awarded to Sonia by His Majesty for her heroic work in caring for the wounded after an air raid on her village.

Although she had seen nothing more bloody than a cut finger in her nineteen years, Sonia took complete charge of twelve wounded, skillfully treated them for everything from shrapnel wounds to shell shock.

"It was nothing," she says modestly now. "So many people have done so much more than I have without winning any medals."

Many people have done more, but few have ever done anything as efficiently as Sonia with as little training as she had. Up to the time of the raid she had attended only two first-aid lectures—one on how to deal with a hemorrhage, the other a verbal explanation of different types of bandages. She had no practical demonstrations and had never unrolled a bandage in her life, but the military doctors and A.R.P. medical experts who inspected her work after the casualties had been taken to hospital refused to believe that she was not a trained nurse.

She had enrolled for A.R.P. work only two months before the raid took place and began her training with an assignment to report every Sunday morning and evening, but before long the eight wardens who man the post in shifts found Sonia volunteering for duty every evening.

X has two military objectives, separated by a half-mile of flimsy lower-middle-class houses and small shops. On a quiet Sunday afternoon in September the Nazis singled out the village for attention. There were nine raiders, Messerschmitt fighters converted to carry four light bombs each.

＋

This is Sonia's story: I had been on duty from ten until noon that Sunday and was just having a cup of tea after my lunch at home when the sirens blew. I wasn't supposed to go on duty again until evening, but most of the wardens report to the post as soon as they hear the sirens.

I bicycled down to the dugout, which is about a quarter of a mile from home. I didn't hear any bombs drop, but there were plenty of planes somewhere overhead, and I could hear the high drone coming closer and closer as I reached the post. I had just propped my bike against the wall of sandbags outside and gone down the steps into the dugout when one of the wardens, Bert Gorrell, who was on duty outside, yelled to some of the others, "Get under cover!" He had seen the first bombs start to drop, but they fell almost half a mile away. Others followed in quick succession. It was horrible to sit in the dugout and hear the bombs exploding nearer and nearer to us. It was all over in a matter of seconds, I suppose, but it seemed hours before the last deafening reverberations died away. The last three bombs were pretty close, about thirty yards down the road.

With the other wardens who had taken shelter in the dugout, I groped my way upstairs and out to the street. The air was filled with fine dust particles and the fumes of exploded bombs, but through it I could see Bert jump on his bicycle and go off down the street. In his excitement he had forgotten to take along the post's two first-aid boxes, which he's supposed to carry with him during a raid. I got them out of the dugout and, carrying one under each handlebar, cycled off after him.

I hadn't gone very far down the road when I heard children screaming. I threw my bike down at the roadside—that was the last I saw of it all day, for I forgot it in the confusion later—and climbed over a huge pile of bricks and timber. A little house had received a direct hit, and the pile was all that was left of it. The screams seemed to come from the back of the house, where I could see an Anderson shelter, with its front entrance pretty badly smashed. Inside, by the light of my torch, I found two little kiddies lying on the floor, with their mother sprawled on top of them. I discovered later that she had tried to protect them with her body as the blast blew in the front of their shelter.

She was covered with blood from bad shrapnel wounds in the head and face. I was just wondering how I could lift her out of the shelter when Bert appeared. Together we carried the woman out onto her washing green in the back yard. The children were unhurt and stopped screaming as soon as we lifted their mother off them. Bert asked me if I could take care of her wounds, since he had to go on further down the road to see if there were more casualties. I said I would do what I could. I suppose I was pretty scared, more with the responsibility than anything else, but I don't remember anything about it now. I just opened one of the first-aid boxes and grabbed the first roll of bandages I put my hands on and did up the woman's head.

Just as I finished, Bert came back. There were no other wounded on this street, so he suggested that I run back to the post and ask them to send the mobile hospital unit (a camouflaged converted bus) along to pick up my injured woman. That was the last I saw of Bert until evening.

With all these bombs dropping, I was sure there must be more injured somewhere, so I started off up the road toward a barracks. Just as I reached the barracks gates, a military policeman ran out and asked me if I could do anything for some civilians whom the soldiers had rescued from some of the bombed buildings. I said I'd do anything to help, but I warned him that I wasn't a trained nurse.

He led me back of the military church, where the soldiers had eleven wounded, mostly women and children, laid out in a long row on the grass. I could see that my two little boxes of first-aid equipment wouldn't last very long, so I told the military policeman and some of the soldiers to fetch me some bandages and water. They were Regular Army veterans, and they looked a little surprised at first when I ordered them about, but they soon brought me everything I needed—except hot water. There was no hot water anywhere in the barracks, so I just had to work with cold.

At one end of the line on the lawn was an old lady—she must have been about seventy—and she had bomb-splinter wounds in the head, arms, and legs. She was absolutely marvelous. When I knelt beside her she objected as loudly as she could, and insisted that I take care of all the others first. But I couldn't leave her. All the while I bandaged her she smiled and talked away. Next to her lay a tiny baby, not more than a year old, all covered with blood and dirt. She kept kicking her legs and waving her arms, so I knew she couldn't be badly injured. When I started to wash her in cold water she cried, but all the blood washed off. It had come from the body of her mother, who had been killed protecting her.

One injured man had me stumped. The soldiers said he was suffering from shell shock, but I had no idea what to do for him. He was lying, dazed, on the grass. Then I suddenly remembered hearing in one of the lectures that if everything else failed a cup of hot sweet stimulant often did wonders. I sent a batman into the officers' mess for a cup of strong hot tea, and told him not to spare the sugar. I was pretty pleased when it worked, and the man was able to stretch out comfortably on the grass.

By the time I had tended to these injured, I must have been a pretty bad mess myself. My slacks and jumper—I didn't even have a warden's uniform at that time—were coated with blood and my arms were grimy up to the elbows. I tried to keep my hands clean, but it wasn't easy with cold water and constant jumping from one person to another. Fortunately for me, some of the injured were suffering only from bad bruises on the head and shoulders, caused by falling debris, and I was able to get them lying easily without attention. Almost as soon as I had finished bandaging the last person, the mobile hospital bus swung in the gates. There was only room for the badly wounded, so the soldiers and the stretcher-bearers lifted them into the bus, and I took three or four who could still walk and led them down the road to the hospital, which was only about 250 yards away. As soon as I saw them taken care of there, I rushed back to the post.

Everything was pretty quiet by then, and Bert and the other wardens were trying to get their reports made out. I settled back to enjoy a cigarette—I don't smoke much, but I certainly needed one then—when the phone rang in the dugout. I answered, and it was the A.R.P. Report Center at the other end asking whether any of the wardens had news of a Mrs. Pratt. Her daughter had been away from Caterham for the day and had just returned to find her mother's home was in the middle of a street roped off because of the presence of delayed-action bombs. The wardens had not listed a Mrs. Pratt among the wounded or those rescued from bombed houses, so Bert and I walked through the village to the Mental Home, where some of the temporary homeless were quartered. But we couldn't find a trace of her there, and her neighbors were afraid that she was still in her house. The house next to hers had been hit and demolished, but we decided that there was a chance that she was still alive.

The military refused to let us pass the barrier and go into the street, because they weren't sure when the time bomb would explode.

We argued and argued, but the soldiers had their orders not to let anyone through, so we went back to the barracks and found the officer in charge. After insisting that we would go into the street entirely on our own risk, he agreed to let us pass the barrier, and even sent another military policeman along to help us search. It was pretty late in the evening by this time, about eleven, I imagine, but we made our way back to X. Just as we reached the barrier, the sirens sounded. Bert wanted me to go back home, where we have an Anderson shelter, or at least to the warden's post, but I wanted to stay on the job until the woman had been found. I knew what her daughter was going through, not knowing whether her mother was dead or alive.

A minute after the sirens sounded we could hear planes overhead, but they appeared to be heading in for London. Anyway, we hoped they wouldn't bother us again that night.

When we reached the house next door to Mrs. Pratt's there was nothing but a gaping hole in the row of houses. Part of the Pratt bungalow had been torn down, but we climbed over the blasted-down front door and picked our way into the hall. Bert said he'd look in the living room, and asked the military policeman to search the kitchen and scullery. I went on down the hall toward the bedroom. I flashed my torch quickly around the room, but saw nothing. Furniture was toppled over and the rugs had been picked up and flung against the walls by the blast. Bert and the soldier called out that they couldn't find her, either.

I went further into the bedroom for another look. The bed was jammed against the wall in one corner, but, just in chance, I got down on my knees and flashed the torch under the bed. Mrs. Pratt was crumpled up in the corner. Bert and the soldier pulled her from under the bed and found she was dead. I had never seen a dead person before, and it was a pretty ghastly sight all right, but I don't think I turned a hair. When I got home afterward and sat in the shelter before going to bed, I did think how horrible the whole day had been.

I Fought over London

by

PILOT OFFICER JOHN M. B. BEARD, D.F.M.

XIII. I FOUGHT OVER LONDON

THERE is no greater glory than that won by the out-numbered young fighter pilots of the R.A.F. who beat back time after time the assaults of the Luft-waffe on the capital of Britain. This is the story of one of them.

He is tall, dark, soft-spoken, twenty-one-year-old Pilot Officer John Maurice Bentley Beard, D.F.M. Beard left Leamington College four years ago to take a job in a bank. While working there he became interested in flying and, like thousands of other young Britons, joined the R.A.F. Volunteer Reserve for flying training during his weekends.

He was called up for active service with a Hurricane squadron posted to the London defense area on the Friday before the outbreak of war. He was in action almost continually during the intensive aerial blitzkrieg on London and won his D.F.M. for destroying a confirmed total of eight machines—three M.E. 110 fighters, the rest bombers—over the capital. He was married shortly after the start of the war.

The action in Beard's story took place during one of the fiercest days of the blitzkrieg, a day in which the Germans claimed to have flung more than one thousand planes against the London area.

This is his story: I was supposed to be away on a day's leave but dropped back to the airdrome to see if there was a letter from my wife. When I found out that *all* the squadrons had gone off into action, I decided to stand by, because obviously something big was happening. While I was climbing into my flying kit, our Hurricanes came slipping back out of the sky to refuel, reload ammunition, and take off again. The returning pilots were full of talk about flocks of enemy bombers and fighters which were trying to break through along the Thames Estuary. You couldn't miss hitting them, they said. Off to the east I could hear the steady roll of anti-aircraft fire. It was a brilliant afternoon with a flawless blue sky. I was crazy to be off.

An instant later an aircraftsman rushed up with orders for me to make up a flight with some of the machines then reloading. My own Hurricane was a nice old kite, though it had a habit of flying left wing low at the slightest provocation. But since it had already accounted for fourteen German aircraft before I inherited it, I thought it had some luck, and I was glad when I squeezed myself into the same old seat again and grabbed the "stick."

We took off in two flights [six fighters], and as we started to gain height over the station we were told over the R.T. [radiotelephone] to keep circling for a while until we were made up to a stronger force. That didn't take long, and soon there was a complete squadron [twelve machines] including a couple of Spitfires which had wandered in from somewhere.

Then came the big thrilling moment: ACTION ORDERS. Distantly I heard the hum of the generator in my R.T. earphones and then the voice of the ground controller crackling through with the call signs. Then the order: "Fifty plus bombers, one hundred plus fighters over Canterbury at 15,000 heading northeast. Your vector [steering course to intercept] nine zero degrees. Over!"

We were flying in four V formations of three. I was flying No. 3 in Red flight, which was the squadron leader's and thus the leading flight. On we went, wing tips to left and right slowly rising and falling, the roar of our twelve Merlins drowning all other sound. We crossed over London, which, at 20,000 feet, seemed just a haze of smoke from its countless chimneys, with nothing visible except the faint glint of the barrage balloons and the wriggly silver line of the Thames.

I had too much to do watching the instruments and keeping formation to do much thinking. But once I caught a reflected glimpse of myself in the windscreen—a goggled, bloated, fat thing with the tube of my oxygen supply protruding gruesomely sideways from the mask which hid my mouth. Suddenly I was back at school again, on a hot afternoon when the Headmaster was taking the Sixth and droning on and on about the later Roman Emperors. The boy on my right was showing me surreptitiously some illustrations which he had pinched out of his father's medical books during the last holidays. I looked like one of those pictures.

It was an amazingly vivid memory, as if school was only yesterday. And half my mind was thinking what wouldn't I then have given to be sitting in a Hurricane belting along at 350 miles an hour and out for a kill. *Me* defending London! I grinned at my old self at the thought.

Minutes went by. Green fields and roads were now beneath us. I scanned the sky and the horizon for the first glimpse of the Germans. A new vector came through on the R.T. and we swung round with the sun behind us. Swift on the heels of this I heard Yellow flight leader call through the earphones. I looked quickly toward Yellow's position, and there *they* were!

It was really a terrific sight and quite beautiful. First they seemed just a cloud of light as the sun caught the many glistening chromium parts of their engines, their windshields, and the spin of their airscrew discs. Then, as our squadron hurtled nearer, the details stood out. I could see the bright-yellow noses of Messerschmitt fighters sandwiching the bombers, and could even pick out some of the types. The sky seemed full of them, packed in layers thousands of feet deep. They came on steadily, wavering up and down along the horizon. "Oh, golly," I thought, "golly, golly . . ."

And then any tension I had felt on the way suddenly left me. I was elated but very calm. I leaned over and switched on my reflector sight, flicked the catch on the gun button from "Safe" to "Fire," and lowered my seat till the circle and dot on the reflector sight shone darkly red in front of my eyes.

The squadron leader's voice came through the earphones, giving tactical orders. We swung round in a great circle to attack on their beam—into the thick of them. Then, on the order, down we went. I took my hand from the throttle lever so as to get both hands on the stick, and my thumb played neatly across the gun button. You have to steady a fighter just as you have to steady a rifle before you fire it.

My Merlin screamed as I went down in a steeply banked dive on to the tail of a forward line of Heinkels. I knew the air was full of aircraft flinging themselves about in all directions, but, hunched and snuggled down behind my sight, I was conscious only of the Heinkel I had picked out. As the angle of my dive increased, the enemy machine loomed larger in the sight field, heaved toward the red dot, and then he was there!

I had an instant's flash of amazement at the Heinkel proceeding so regularly on its way with a fighter on its tail. "Why doesn't the fool *move?*" I thought, and actually caught myself flexing my muscles into the action *I* would have taken had I been he.

When he was square across the sight I pressed the button. There was a smooth trembling of my Hurricane as the eight-gun squirt shot out. I gave him a two-second burst and then another. Cordite fumes blew back into the cockpit, making an acrid mixture with the smell of hot oil and the air-compressors.

I saw my first burst go in and, just as I was on top of him and turning away, I noticed a red glow inside the bomber. I turned tightly into position again and now saw several short tongues of flame lick out along the fuselage. Then he went down in a spin, blanketed with smoke and with pieces flying off.

I left him plummeting down and, horsing back on my stick, climbed up again for more. The sky was clearing, but ahead toward London I saw a small, tight formation of bombers completely encircled by a ring of Messerschmitts. They were still heading north. As I raced forward, three flights of Spitfires came zooming up from beneath them in a sort of Prince-of-Wales's-feathers maneuver. They burst through upward and outward, their guns going all the time. They must have each got one, for an instant later I saw the most extraordinary sight of eight German bombers and fighters diving earthward together in flames.

I turned away again and streaked after some distant specks ahead. Diving down, I noticed that the running progress of the battle had brought me over London again. I could see the network of streets with the green space of Kensington Gardens, and I had an instant's glimpse of the Round Pond, where I sailed boats when I was a child. In that moment, and as I was rapidly overhauling the Germans ahead, a Dornier 17 sped right across my line of flight, closely pursued by a Hurricane. And behind the Hurricane came two Messerschmitts. He was too intent to have seen them and they had not seen me! They were coming slightly toward me. It was perfect. A kick at the rudder and I swung in toward them, thumbed the gun button, and let them have it. The first burst was placed just the right distance ahead of the leading Messerschmitt. He ran slap into it and he simply came to pieces in the air. His companion, with one of the speediest and most brilliant "get-outs" I have ever seen, went right away in a half Immelmann turn. I missed him completely. He must almost have been hit by the pieces of the leader but he got away. I hand it to him.

At that moment some instinct made me glance up at my rear-view mirror and spot two Messerschmitts closing in on my tail. Instantly I hauled back on the stick and streaked upward. And just in time. For as I flicked into the climb, I saw the tracer streaks pass beneath me. As I turned I had a quick look round the "office" [cockpit]. My fuel reserve was running out and I had only about a second's supply of ammunition left. I was certainly in no condition to take on two Messerschmitts. But they seemed no more eager than I was. Perhaps they were in the same position, for they turned away for home. I put my nose down and did likewise.

Only on the way back did I realize how hot I was. I had forgotten to adjust the ventilator apparatus in all the stress of the fighting, and hadn't noticed the thermometer. With the sun on the windows all the time, the inside of the "office" was like an oven. Inside my flying suit I was in a bath of perspiration, and sweat was cascading down my face. I was dead tired and my neck ached from constantly turning my head on the lookout when going in and out of dogfights. Over east the sky was flecked with A.A. puffs, but I did not bother to investigate. Down I went, home.

At the station there was only time for a few minutes' stretch, a hurried report to the Intelligence Officer, and a brief comparing of notes with the other pilots. So far my squadron seemed to be intact, in spite of a terrific two hours in which we had accounted for at least thirty enemy aircraft.

But there was more to come. It was now about 4 P.M., and I gulped down some tea while the ground crews checked my Hurricane. Then, with about three flights collected, we took off again. We seemed to be rather longer this time circling and gaining height above the station before the orders came through on the R.T. It was to patrol an area along the Thames Estuary at 20,000 feet. But we never got there.

We had no sooner got above the docks than we ran into the first lot of enemy bombers. They were coming up in line about 5,000 feet below us. The line stretched on and on across the horizon. Above, on our level, were assorted groups of enemy fighters. Some were already in action, with our fellows spinning and twirling among them. Again I got that tightening feeling at the throat, for it really was a sight to make you gasp.

But we all knew what to do. We went for the bombers. Kicking her over, I went down after the first of them, a Heinkel 111. He turned away as I approached, chiefly because some of our fellows had already broken into the line and had scattered it. Before I got up he had been joined by two more. They were forming a V and heading south across the river.

I went after them. Closing in on the tail of the left one, I ran into a stream of cross fire from all three. How it missed me I don't know. For a second the whole air in front was thick with tracer trails. It seemed to be coming straight at me, only to curl away by the windows and go lazily past. I felt one slight bank, however, and glancing quickly, saw a small hole at the end of my starboard wing. Then, as the Heinkel drifted across my sights, I pressed the button—once —twice . . . Nothing happened.

I panicked for a moment till I looked down and saw that I had forgotten to turn the safety-catch knob to the "Fire" position. I flicked it over at once and in that instant saw that three bombers, to hasten their getaway, had jettisoned all their bombs. They seemed to peel off in a steady stream. We were over the southern outskirts of London now and I remember hoping that most of them would miss the little houses and plunge into fields.

But dropping the bombs did not help my Heinkel. I let him have a long burst at close range, which got him right in the "office." I saw him turn slowly over and go down, and followed to give him another squirt. Just then there was a terrific crash in front of me. Something flew past my window, and the whole aircraft shook as the engine raced itself to pieces. I had been hit by A.A. fire aimed at the bombers, my airscrew had been blown off, and I was going down in a spin.

The next few seconds were a bit wild and confused. I remember switching off and flinging back the sliding roof almost in one gesture. Then I tried to vault out through the roof. But I had forgotten to release my safety belt. As I fumbled at the pin the falling aircraft gave a twist which shot me through the open cover. Before I was free, the air stream hit me like a solid blow and knocked me sideways. I felt my arm hit something, and then I was falling over and over with fields and streets and sky gyrating madly past my eyes.

I grabbed at the rip cord on my chute. Missed it. Grabbed

again. Missed it. That was no fun. Then I remember saying to myself, "This won't do. Take it easy, take it slowly." I tried again and found the rip cord grip and pulled. There was a terrific wrench at my thighs and then I was floating still and peacefully with my "brolly" canopy billowing above my head.

The rest was lovely. I sat at my ease just floating gradually down, breathing deep, and looking around. I was drifting across London again at about 2,000 feet. Just below me I spotted another parachute, a German, probably from the bomber I had shot down. I shouted to him but he did not appear to hear me. He was about 500 feet lower and falling faster than me.

I drifted toward the river. Lower now, and over the crowded dockland area I could plainly see the wreck of houses which the bombers had left in their wake and the smoke of fires. At one point I could actually see fire engines hurtling along a street. There was no other traffic visible. The northward fringe of London's houses came nearer. I could see that I had plenty of room to miss the crowded roofs and land in open fields.

I actually landed in an allotment garden, my trailing body and the parachute harness simply massacring whole rows of runner beans. I brought up finally in a compost heap, festooned with tendrils and the peas and beans I dragged with me.

I lay there for a minute or two, just glad to be alive. In that short while a whole posse of Home Guards and air-raid wardens burst into the allotment and surrounded me. I think I was a little bit screwy, because I just lay there and smiled at them, although they were looking so wary and ferocious. Nice, ordinary little blokes. I could have kissed them.

Then I said, "Help me out of this harness, will you?" I found I could not move my right arm, which hurt a lot from that bump I felt as I had baled out. They obliged cheerfully, handling me as carefully as if I were made of glass. I started to say how sorry I was that I had made such a mess of the runner beans when someone stuck a cigarette in my mouth.

They helped me to get my tunic off while I had a look at my arm. It wasn't bad. My shoulder was out a bit and that was all, except for a few bruises on my leg. We walked in a procession to the allotment entrance, where the chief warden said his car was waiting. By coincidence I had landed only three or four miles from my own station, and the warden offered to drive me there. But just as we got to the road an ambulance drove up. "That's service for you," said one of the wardens. So I had to climb in and be driven back to the station medical officer. I was minus my Hurricane, I had a slightly damaged shoulder, but I was plus two German bombers and a fighter. It was the end of a perfect day.

I Bombed the Barges

by

THE CAPTAIN OF A BLENHEIM BOMBER

XIV. I BOMBED THE BARGES

THE narrator is a twenty-eight-year-old Scot who has raided nearly all the invasion ports, from Flushing to Brest, on some night or another since the first British onslaught began in early September.

If anything, Air Ministry bulletins have minimized the scale and intensity of these R.A.F. attacks, which went on from twilight to dawn without intermission until the last week of October. The imminence of the invasion threat probably inspired the sustained ferocity of the raids. They have laid waste every port and harbor from Holland to the Atlantic seaboard of France and smashed all German hopes of a landing in Britain and an early conclusion to the war. Air power—the battering ram of the Luftwaffe—brought the German Army to the Channel ports; air power—the might of the R.A.F.—stopped it there.

Since the British expected to find considerable fighter opposition at these ports, Blenheim bombers were used in preference to heavy night bombers like the Wellingtons, Whitleys, and Hampdens. The R.A.F. has plenty of Blenheims, which are fighter-bombers and which could more than make up in speed and maneuverability what they might sacrifice in sheer load capacity.

As it happened, the R.A.F. found little fighter opposition. But according to the pilots, the ground defenses were hotter than anything encountered in their raids over German territory. It is believed that large numbers of mobile A.A. batteries were taken away from home defense in Germany and packed around the Channel ports. At any rate, pilots on "sorties" into Germany reported a much easier time while the bombing of the barges was proceeding. In addition, most of the A.A. guns and ammunition captured from the French, Belgians, and Dutch were packed into the restricted areas round these ports. And the Blenheim's special qualities of speed and "handling" came in useful in facing and breaking through such a hell-fire of ground defense.

The nickname given by bomber crews to the coastline of the invasion ports is "Blackpool Front." Blackpool, in Lancashire, is Britain's Coney Island, famous in prewar days for grandiose illuminations and firework spectacles.

The pilot who tells this story is a rather rangy young man with a droll sense of humor and speech full of telling metaphors. Before the war he was a constructional engineer employed in his father's firm, which has built, among other things, most of the cinemas for a big group in Britain.

He is a completely professional type and grimly deplores the exigencies of this war, which has brought him to "knocking things down when I would rather be building them up." But apparently he can do both equally well.

This is the Captain's story: It was three o'clock in the morning. An hour before, I was sleeping peacefully in my warm bed at the airdrome; now I was encased in noisy, vibrating metal walls, rumbling southeast under the stars over the dark, hidden fields and sleeping villages of England. At 9,000 feet I turned on my oxygen supply and instructed my rear gunner and the bomb-aimer to do likewise. It was freezing-cold and we've learned from experience that oxygen helps warm the blood.

We were heading for Ostend. As I watched the vague, greenish glimmer from the radium-painted instrument dials, I ran over in my mind all that we had been told at the "briefing" that evening. Again I visualized the photograph which our Intelligence Officer had shown us: the rows of 100-foot barges, ten in a line, ten rows deep, lying in each of the four harbor basins. From the height at which the picture was taken, they looked like matchsticks loosely bundled together.

I again pictured the three arms of the jetties separating the basins, three black lines jutting out toward the harbor entrance and probably packed with military stores and men. But it was the barges I was after, and I began to review our method of attack. I decided I would not bomb up the basins. If I was even a tiny bit out, my bombs might miss the water space and hit the jetties. No, I would bomb diagonally across all four basins. Then *some* of the stick of bombs would be certain to hit barges.

I thought of my chances of getting in for a low attack without being spotted. They were good, because I was the leading aircraft of my squadron. The others were following me at three-minute intervals and behind them were squadrons from two other stations. It was to be a proper "do." We were to put Ostend out of the invasion business for some time to come.

But since I would be the first visitor that night, I hoped that the usual "reception committee" would not be at work and that I would be able to throttle back well out to sea and glide in unobserved. I knew some of our boys had been busy already at Dunkirk and Calais, but I still hoped that the panic there would not have affected the German gunners at Ostend.

Reflecting about these matters, I began to get a little worried. It was pitch black outside, but I wondered whether even the faint glow from the instrument panels would affect our vision. I'm a stickler on this subject of darkness. I won't have any light at all inside my aircraft on a night raid. It's not that we might be spotted by enemy watchers but that I need about twenty minutes to get my full night vision and the slightest glint of light puts me off for another twenty minutes. And if we were to make a surprise attack, both the bomb-aimer and I would have to be at our best to pick up the target and the outline of the jetties on such a moonless night. And it would have to be done almost instantly after we crossed the enemy coastline. If we didn't pick it up and bomb at once, I would have to open up the motors again for another run on to the barges. Then the band would begin to play and low bombing would be out of the question.

Just then my navigator switched on his shrouded hand torch to scan the map on his table. He sits in front of me and the table is hidden from my view by my instrument panel, but a tiny reflected glow touched the side windows of the cabin. I told him urgently to hurry with his position check and douse the torch, and then kicked myself for being so brusque. He was a good bomb-aimer, quick, calm and accurate, and this was his last trip with me, as he was leaving the squadron to go on a pilot's course. A good bomb-aimer makes all the difference in getting your job done quickly and successfully and getting the hell out of it. I was fed up at losing him, so I chatted to him mildly for a while about various details.

We were over the sea now, heading for Ostend. I could tell that by the different sound of the motors, which always change their note over the sea. I did the last-minute jobs, setting the bomb fuses and pressing down the bomb-selection switches so the packets would all leave in a stick. It won't be long now, I thought, settling down in the seat.

I put her up in a long, slow climb to 15,000, at which height I would begin my glide in from about ten miles out. I warned my navigator to make a close check on our speed and course so that he could tell me the right moment to throttle back and start down.

Halfway across the Channel, I saw the glow of fires, the flash of bombs, bursting shells, and a great cascade of tracers, "flaming onions," and other muck coming up on my right along the French coast, where other British bombers were hitting hard. But to my left and straight ahead there was complete darkness. "Still good," I thought, and concentrated on my flying and the instruments. The navigator left his bench and squatted forward over the bomb sight. He began to check various readings with me over the phones. Just then my rear gunner, perched in his lonely cubbyhole amidships, called out "Fighter!" I listened anxiously through the crackle of the phones. Then the direction. "Red [port beam] below." Instantly I kicked the rudder over and climbed, so as to give the gunner a fair go at it. I leveled and waited. Then the gunner again: "He's out of range. But he's seen us. He's stalking us, sir."

There was nothing to do but go down again and turn widely off course, hoping to lose him. For it was no use attempting to argue with him. I had a job to do. Meanwhile I made rapid calculations. If I did not shake him off quickly, all my plans for a silent approach to the barges would be upset and the following aircraft from my squadron would be on top of me. I thumped the handle of my stick with impatience. We dived, swerved, swung around again, and hoped for the best. As luck would have it, my gunner soon announced that the fighter had gone. I got back on my course, giving full throttle to make up for lost time.

The whole of "Blackpool Front" was now in near view. It was an amazing spectacle. The Calais docks were on fire. So was the waterfront of Boulogne, and glares extended for miles. The whole French coast seemed to be a barrier of flame broken only by intense white flashes of exploding bombs and varicolored incendiary tracers soaring and circling skyward.

The rear gunner, who had hardly uttered a word throughout the entire trip, was shouting excitedly through the "intercom." "Gawd! Look at that—and that!" I grinned to myself as he went burbling on. He never talks as a rule, never complains or tries to open up a line of gossip, as many rear gunners do, afflicted by the loneliness and cold of their job.

Throughout many a raid he has spoken to me only when he has had to answer routine questions. As he once put it to me with a grin, "Sometimes I sits and thinks, and sometimes I just sits."

We were getting near now. But not a peep, not a glimmer from the darkness ahead. I made some last-minute adjustments and called to the navigator, who called out "Now!"

I throttled back and put the nose down. Pressing my head against the windows, I strained and peered out to pick up the first glimpse of the Ostend harbor works. The navigator had gone forward to squat over his bomb sight in the nose. The semi-silence after the steady roar of the motors was almost startling. The air stream rushing past us rose in a high, steady, whistling scream as we plunged down. I thought of the waiting gun crews hidden there far ahead in the darkness, the massed soldiers on the quays and in the barges, unaware of our coming. I felt exultant, tremendous. I felt like singing above the vast avenging crescendo of my bomber driving through the sky.

And then I thought, "They'll hear us! They'll hear us!" The drone of the motors was cut, but the scream of the air stream was now deafening. The Blenheim was trembling as we touched the top speed of the dive. In that instant the navigator called, "Left, left!" As I obeyed instantly with rudder pressure, I saw the harbor too—a black outline on the darkness. It rushed nearer and upward. "Steady! Ri-i-ght! Steady!" chanted the bomb-aimer. We were over the harbor front. I fought the stick, flickering my gaze to ground and back to the quivering altimeter needle. Down to 500. There were the four jetty arms. We were dead on line. A search-light shot up to the right of us, miles out and too late. I had an instant's thought of my bomb-aimer crouched forward with his hand on the lever of the "Mickey Mouse" [R.A.F. slang for bomb-release device], his eyes glued on those barge-filled basins sliding down between the drift wires on the bomb sight. Then came the great, surging kick on the stick as the bombs left the plane. A second later he was through to me on the phones and calmly announced, "Bombs gone."

My waiting hand threw open the throttle levers in a flash. The motors thundered out. Hauling back on the stick, kick-ing at the rudder, we went up in a great, banking climb. As we went, I stared down and out through the windows. There they were! One, two, three, four vast flashes as my bombs struck. In the light of the last one, just as lightning will sud-denly paint a whole landscape, I saw the outline of the jetties in vivid relief. Between them the water boiled with thin black shapes. They were barges flung end up and fragments turn-ing slowly over and over in the air.

Then came a most gigantic crash. We were nearly 2,000 feet up now and well away from the jetties, but the whole aircraft pitched over, as if a giant blow had struck us underneath. A vivid flash enveloped us and lingered, as sound burst round our ears. It was a blinding white flash like a great sheet of daylight stuck in between the dark. While all hell broke loose round us, I fought like mad to get control of the bomber. But all the time my mind was blankly wondering—half stunned as I was—what the devil had we hit. Afterward I learned that the last bomb had struck a group of mines stacked on a jetty waiting to be loaded aboard the mine-layers. Photographs taken the next morning showed two stone jetties blown away to the water's edge, all barges vanished from the inner basins, and devastation over a mile radius!

Then the searchlights got me. I plunged inland to dodge them, but they held, and the sky all round us was packed with every kind of muck arching over us and all around. It was a bad few minutes, and once or twice I thought we would never get out. In their mass of colored bursts the flak [German anti-aircraft fire] was crazily beautiful but horrible. The whole interior of my aircraft was lit up. I saw my navigator sitting up at my feet rubbing his head. He had been flung out of his compartment when we turned over in that great explosion.

There was a new kind of fiery flak which followed us and stuck close on either side. It resembled the three colored balls of a pawnbroker's sign. They frightened me. I watched them diving and climbing wildly, and dodged as best I could. They were probably clues to my position for their fighters, but they looked damnably dangerous. Somehow—I don't know how—we were out. I turned again and headed out to sea. Taking stock of ourselves, I called up the rear gunner. "I'm O.K.," he said, "but I didn't expect a ride in a rocket." My navigator said that he had been laid out when he was flung at my feet, but all he had now was a bad headache. Turning again along the coast, I saw more and more great flashes as others of my squadron went into Ostend. The whole sky was packed with A.A. bursts and I counted twenty great fires at different places round the harbor. Against the flames, the whole town stood out clearly. Most of the squadron, I reflected, would have had a free run in from the sea while the batteries were concentrating on me inland. In the din of that first great explosion their approaching engines would not have been heard. They couldn't have wished for a brighter target.

Then we swung around and headed for home. Behind us, yet another of the German Army's invasion ports was a bonfire on the skyline. The dawn was coming up across my right shoulder. England lay in her guarded sleep just ahead of us. The engines droned on. We were tired but somehow peaceful and happy as we quietly munched our rations.

Coventry Doctor

by

DR. HARRY WINTER

XV. COVENTRY DOCTOR

ON THE night of November 14, the German Luftwaffe singled out the industrial city of Coventry for the first of its mass terror raids on Britain. In the twelve-hour bombardment that ensued, a small group of doctors and nurses worked all night in the Coventry and Warwickshire Hospital, main casualty center for the region. They lacked heat and power; they suffered five direct hits and by dawn their building was a windowless ruin. The story of this frightful, heroic night is told by a twenty-eight-year-old Canadian, Dr. Harry Winter, chief surgeon of the hospital.

I had just finished an operation and was on my way down to the surgeons' dining room for dinner when the Coventry warning siren sounded. It was about seven. We get everything in readiness as soon as the alert goes, but we don't go to our action stations until the sound of gunfire or bombs dropping tells us that danger is imminent. I hoped to have enough time to enjoy my meal, but I had just dipped into my soup when I heard the first whishing downward rush of a bomb. We'd had occasional raids before, but somehow I had a premonition that this was going to be a bad one, and as I went to the wall to switch on the yellow action-station lights throughout the hospital, I remember saying to the other surgeons, "Well, fellows, I feel we're going to get it tonight."

My own action station is to patrol the wards and corridors just to see that everything is shipshape. I walked through the maternity ward from the dining room and noticed that all the patients had been placed under their beds, with their mattresses over the top of them. Nurses were wheeling other beds down from the top floors and lining them along the ground-floor corridors, away from flying glass. Since we haven't any underground rooms, that's the best protection we can offer.

I went on up three flights of stairs and stepped out onto the flat roof of the main building. I could hardly believe my eyes. All around the hospital grounds glowed literally hundreds of incendiary bombs, like lights twinkling on a mammoth Christmas tree. Down below, in the light of other fires which were already lighting up the sky over the city, I could see the men of the hospital staff running from bomb to bomb, dousing them with buckets of sand. I heard later that some of the male patients spent most of the night in the grounds putting out incendiaries.

Half a dozen small fires had already started in the hospital buildings, flames were licking through the roof of the laundry, and another blaze was going on the roof of the emergency storeroom next door to it. From the roof, the hospital superintendent was shouting instructions to the hospital's auxiliary fire crew down below, and before long they had their hoses going on both buildings. As we watched, however, flames leaped from the roof of the main storeroom. We were pretty worried by this time, for fires in both storerooms might destroy all our supplies except those on hand in the hospital, just enough for a normal night's work.

I left them fighting the fires and went down to check up on the reception building, where the casualties would arrive. Everyone was waiting tensely, but the preparations had been completed smoothly. Voluntary stretcher-bearers, supplied by the St. John's Ambulance Corps, had laid out wooden trestles ready for the stretchers which would be brought in the ambulances. The reception officer, a Coventry surgeon who had waited night after night for just such an emergency, was ready to give each incoming patient a preliminary examination before tagging him for the type of treatment required in the wards or operating rooms.

I had just about completed my inspection when the real fun started. First, an incendiary fell on the roof of the nurses' home. Fortunately, a workman examining the roof the day before had put his foot through a rotten section and the hole had not been repaired. A nurse passing along the top-floor corridor happened to look up and saw the incendiary perched on the edge of the hole. She gave the alarm and the fire was put out before it could get hold, but we decided to evacuate the building and bring all the nurses into the main section. Again we were lucky. No sooner had the last nurse left the building than a heavy explosive crashed into it and exploded on the thick concrete top floor. That was our first direct hit.

About eight-thirty, another shower of incendiaries started fires on top of the men's medical ward, the women's medical ward, and the eye ward. With the other surgeons, the orderlies and nurses, and even some of the able male patients, I ran across the open space between the main building and these wards and began transferring the patients. The nurses wheeled the beds outside while the rest of us hoisted patients on our shoulders and carried them pickaback across to the main hall. There wasn't a murmur from one of them, although some must have been pretty badly hurt with the jogging we gave them. Providence must have been watching over us. As I reached the door of the main building with the last patient on my back, a bomb screamed down and plunged into the men's ward. Instinctively I turned around after the explosion and saw the whole wall of the building fall slowly outward

I BOMBED THE BARGES

BRITISH BOMBER

I BOMBED THE BARGES

BARGES OF GERMANY'S INVASION FLEET

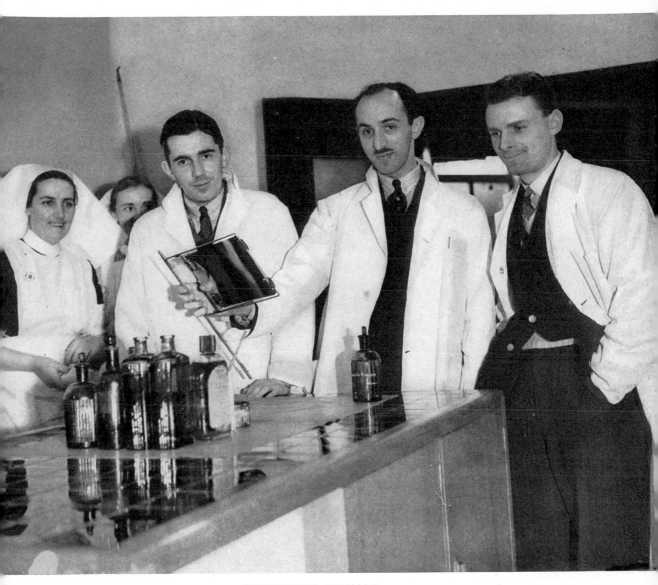

COVENTRY DOCTOR

DR. HARRY WINTER, AND ASSISTANTS, AFTER OPERATING DURING RAID

COVENTRY DOCTOR

RETRIEVING MEDICAL SUPPLIES AFTER RAID

COVENTRY DOCTOR

STREET SCENE

LONDON STANDS UP TO THE BLITZKRIEG

A LIFE IS SAVED

LONDON STANDS UP TO THE BLITZKRIEG

CITY WORKERS FIND THEIR OWN BUSES

LONDON STANDS UP TO THE BLITZKRIEG

WEDDING UNDER FIRE

and crash across the open ground where we had been but a few seconds before.

We put the patients on stretchers and blankets along the main-floor corridors, which were already so crowded that we had to tread carefully to get from one end of the hospital to the other. Then the casualties started to come in from outside. From then on, everything flashed past me like the action in a speeded-up film. I remember assigning the other surgeons to their theaters: I took the main one on the second floor.

We had made elaborate preparations for classifying the patients as they came in, but we didn't have time for detailed examinations. All we could do was to divide them roughly into resuscitation cases and those requiring immediate surgery. The resuscitation patients were whisked into beds and given electric blankets and oxygen, to help them recover from the shock of their wounds. The immediate surgery cases were divided among the three theaters. I suppose I did about fifteen operations throughout the night, some of them more intricate than others, but they came too fast for me to keep count. The other theaters handled about forty.

We couldn't work very rapidly. Wounds are very tricky in this war of bombs. The majority of cases were lacerations or injuries to limbs. The complication with bomb lacerations is that there is a small wound on the surface but extensive disruption underneath. Everything is pulped together. It's no use fixing the surface wound without doing a major cutting job on the inside—and that takes time.

About midnight, the electric power went off, but I continued with the operation I was on by the light from two small bulbs run by our own emergency lighting system. By this time I was feeling pretty shaky, I admit. I wasn't exactly frightened, but the sound of a bomb whistling down from 5,000 to 6,000 feet above you isn't a comfortable one. Every few minutes the nurses and the anesthetist threw themselves under the operating table as the bombs roared down. I didn't like to follow them, but every time one whistled uncomfortably close I instinctively pulled the knife away and ducked sideways.

Whenever I began to think too much of the bombs, however, I thought of the patients lying all over the hospital, just trusting to luck that they would not be hit. Up on the top floor of the gynecological ward we had fifteen women whom we couldn't move. They stayed in their beds through it all without a complaint, although a bomb that smashed the staff quarters next door covered them with glass from their windows and plaster from the ceiling. In another wing we had to leave a dozen fracture cases. All night long they lay on their backs, unable to move, hung up on their frames, and watched the Jerry planes cruising about the fire-lit sky through a huge hole that had been blown out of the wall. The effect was stupefying. Throughout the packed hospital there was not one cry of fear, not one sign of panic. We didn't have a case of hysteria all night long.

The only word of complaint came from a wounded German airman who'd been in the hospital for a few days. He was on the top floor of the main building and I noticed that no one seemed to want to risk his own life to bring him downstairs. When the orderlies finally went to him, they found him cringing in bed and muttering in English. "Too much bomb—too long! Too much bomb!"

By this time the windows in my operating theater had been blasted out and a bitter-cold wind was blowing across the room. It was too cold to uncover the patients and too cold to operate, for I was shivering from head to foot. The windows of the second theater had also been blown out, so we were forced to move into the ground-floor theater, the windows of which were protected from blast by an outside brick wall erected by a farsighted Ministry of Health. It was an amazing scene. It looked far worse than the descriptions I've heard of the front-line casualty clearing stations of the World War.

Patients were lying head to toe on every inch of space. The nurses were marvelous. With hurricane lamps and hand torches they moved about among the patients, comforting them and giving them little sips of water. That was about all we could do for them.

It was bitterly cold throughout the hospital. Most of the windows had been blasted out, walls had been blown down, and not a door remained in its frame. We issued extra blankets to all the patients, but they kept coming in so fast that we didn't have time to make them comfortable. Although we have only 440 beds, we had 275 patients in when the raid started, some of them victims of previous bombings, and I estimate that at least 300 more were admitted during the night.

By 4 A.M. I couldn't keep a steady hand. I had taken nothing to eat except a sip of soup since lunchtime the day before. Then our emergency lighting failed just as I was in the middle of an operation. We quickly rigged up an automobile headlamp to a battery set and I finished the job. Bombs were still crashing down, but by a great miracle the only casualty was a soldier who was lending us a hand. While he was crossing a courtyard, a bomb fell directly on him and blew him to bits.

When daylight finally brought an end to the raid, it was the most welcome dawn I have ever seen—only to be marred when wardens rushed in to report that they had found a delayed-action bomb buried just outside the ground-floor operating theater. All the patients in the main building within range of the bomb had to be evacuated immediately. But no sooner was this done than we got orders to evacuate the whole hospital full of patients to other hospitals in neighboring towns. The ambulance and stretcher men, who had been on their feet and out in the debris-littered streets all night long, worked hour after hour. By five that afternoon, the last ambulance rolled away from the doors and I sat down to my first meal in twenty-eight hours.

We were without power and steam. We had lost hundreds of pounds' worth of supplies when the storerooms were fired and were certainly not in shape to operate, but we didn't feel that our job was finished. That night we had an emergency casualty station set up in the surgeons' dining room, with our instruments boiling in a pan on the fire, just in case Jerry paid Coventry another visit.

London Stands Up to the Blitzkrieg

by

WALTER GRAEBNER

XVI. LONDON STANDS UP TO THE BLITZKRIEG

LONDON is in a state of siege, the outcome of which will probably determine the winner of World War II. For eight months the 6,000,000 inhabitants left in the great, gray city have been living under the terrible threat of invasion by the greatest army on earth, encamped across the English Channel less than 100 miles from Buckingham Palace. Londoners on the southern outskirts of the capital can sometimes even hear the big guns shelling the coastal cities where the Nazis might try to establish bridgeheads. Against the chance of invasion, from all directions at once, the British General Staff have heavily fortified and mined every winding road and broad thoroughfare leading into London. Home Guards and crack troops with machine guns and rifles stand guard twenty-four hours a day at railroad stations, Government buildings, factories, bridges, and other key points. Sandbagged barricades and small concrete forts have been built at all important intersections. Armored cars, Bren gun-carriers, and lorries rumble through the streets continuously while raw British tommies and their allies train in the streets and squares.

Air-raid warnings, bursting bombs, roaring planes, clanging fire engines, and racing ambulances keep the whole town fitfully awake to the endless bombardment from the air. Against the nightmare backdrop of this huge and terrible siege, the life of London continues with calm, incongruous persistence.

Londoners are admirably suited to stand up to the blitzkrieg. Small and wiry, they can slip quickly into low, cramped Anderson shelters and dugouts. Phlegmatic, they express practically no emotion when death and disaster strike near. Unused to a high standard of life, they don't grumble when they lose their homes, their possessions, and their jobs. So long as they can have three or four cups of tea every day and go for walks, their two most cherished desires have been satisfied. Because for centuries they have braved one of the world's worst climates, sturdy Londoners do not find leaky roofs and damp shelters unbearable. Because they've fought so many wars in the past, they don't look upon this war as a calamity, even though it's coming down on top of them.

Nothing that's happened in the war so far has excited Londoners. The Norwegian and Dunkirk evacuations, the fall of France, the R.A.F. victories over the Luftwaffe, the Italian defeats at Taranto, in Greece and Egypt, even the smashing attacks on London and the provincial cities have left them completely unmoved. Londoners find it impossible to work up any hatred for Germany and Italy. Nevertheless the idea of anything but ultimate victory never so much as crosses their minds. If the Reichswehr should contrive to push its way to the very banks of the Thames, Londoners would still proclaim, "The British lose every battle but the last."

In such a frame of mind, Londoners neither keep a balance sheet on the progress of the war nor worry about how it will be won. After the collapse of France they simply, and rather philosophically, said, "We never really expected much from the French anyway. Now we know where we stand." Likewise, average Londoners don't count on United States aid to win the war. If it comes in large quantities, they'll be grateful in a quiet, unemotional way. If it doesn't come, they'll not be discouraged, nor will they show any bitterness toward America. When Londoners can be induced to comment at all on the possibility of United States intervention, they say, "Why should America want to get mixed up in this mess? You're way over there across the ocean and well out of it. We can't expect you to help us deal with Hitler." Whether Londoners realize that Germany represents as serious a threat to America as to the British Empire is a moot question, but one thing is certain: ordinary Londoners would never think of hinting that America should do more than she is already doing to help Britain win the war.

London, even taking into account its enormous size, seems to be able to stand the Luftwaffe's poundings much better than the other cities. Whereas the Nazis can wipe out the heart of a big provincial city in a single night, the center of London still looked pretty normal after at least thirty nights during which bombs rained on it continuously. The John Lewis [department store] section of Oxford Street is the only area in the West End that can be remotely compared with the ruined business districts of Coventry, Bristol, and Southampton.

In the last 90 days no less than 100,000 bombs have fallen on the metropolitan area of London. Of these, probably half were incendiaries, which carry no explosive power but will start raging fires after a few minutes unless they are smothered by sand, blankets, or some similar material. Londoners have become adept at extinguishing them, taught by the dreadful lesson of the September dock fires. About a quarter were HE [high explosive] bombs, weighing anywhere from 25 pounds to 1,000 pounds, which explode immediately on contact with a hard surface. Probably a fifth were time bombs, which go off from three minutes to three days after landing. The rest were land mines—metal cylinders filled with 4,000 pounds of high-explosive material—which float down on parachutes and cause the most damage of all.

206

In the hundred square miles encirling Piccadilly Circus, it would be hard to find more than a few blocks that haven't been hit by at least one bomb. The consequences, however, are less terrible than one might expect. For example, although all thirteen of the city's main railroad terminals are in this area, only one has ever been put out of commission for more than a few hours. The bomb which closed the station actually dropped several miles away—in a street over the main-line tunnel. Likewise, the Germans have failed to hit even one of the many bridges that are concentrated along central London's ten-mile stretch of the Thames. Vital gas, power, and water works in the same area are also still functioning at capacity, though several have been slightly damaged by "near misses." Only a few tube lines or stations have been hit and none seriously enough to cause anything but temporary suspension of services. Most of the factories lie outside the hundred square miles and, like the industrial sections of the provincial cities, have for some curious reason been practically ignored by the German bombers. In a military sense, it has been fortunate for the British that most of the bombs in London have fallen on houses, churches, public buildings, schools, pubs, cinemas, shops, apartment buildings, and open spaces.

Although no more bombs have dropped on the East End than on many other parts of London, the damage there is by far the most extensive. The reason for this is that the East End is one vast sprawling slumland of small, old, closely packed dwellings and shops which topple over like a pack of cards from the force of a bomb. A single land mine is known to have driven 400 families out of their homes.

In the dockland borough of West Ham, which has a population of 300,000, over half of the houses have been rendered uninhabitable. They have either been destroyed completely or require large-scale repairs, which, owing to the war machine's demand for labor and materials, are unobtainable. West Hamites are faced with other problems besides broken houses. Over one-third of the population have no shelters whatever while another quarter have shelters which are half submerged in water. Also, when West Hamites are bombed out, their predicament is far worse than that of the middle or upper classes, who simply go to friends or to hotels. West Hamites must go to public shelters or rest centers because their friends' homes have either been bombed too or are already over-crowded.

West Ham and the other dockland boroughs caught their worst "packets" in the early weeks of the blitz. What was a serious situation from the start became a near-catastrophe because of local bickerings and an unwillingness on the part of borough officials to co-operate with Whitehall administrators. West Hamites still haven't recovered from the shock of the

Horseferry Road school disaster on the Tuesday afternoon of September 10. With much of dockland aflame and bombs crashing all around, about 600 homeless women and children were herded into Horseferry Road School, whence they were to be taken by busses to the countryside. Blundering West Ham officials, however, dispatched the busses to the wrong place, and while the 600 people waited in agony, a 500-pounder landed squarely on top of the school. Only about 50 people were pulled out of the debris alive.

The Horseferry School explosion was the worst single catastrophe of the war in London to date. No official casualty figures have been released, but a roundup of all bombing casualties might reveal 18,000 deaths, 25,000 seriously wounded, and $1,000,000,000 of property damage. Added to this is the intangible factor of confusion. During the worst weeks of September and October, thousands of East End women and children were whisked off to the country before anyone thought to keep records of their names and whereabouts. Ever since, husbands who later returned home from work or from the fighting services on leave have been trying vainly to locate the missing members of their families.

When the blitz on London first started, many people took heart in the belief that a large proportion of the bombs was sure to land in the streets, thus sparing the buildings. This proved to be the case, but for every building spared, a vastly greater price than it represented was paid in damage to sewers and mains, not to speak of the unholy traffic snarls caused by the blocked streets. One single bomb, for example, which landed in Charing Cross Road in front of famed Foyle's book-shops, did $2,500,000 worth of damage to installations under the street. It took a crew of engineers two months to build a bridge over the crater so that this vital thoroughfare could be reopened for traffic. Incidentally, Foyle didn't let the bridge-opening pass without ceremony. Across one end of the bridge he stretched a white ribbon which, in the presence of close friends, he cut at the appointed time. The span is now known as Foyle's Bridge.

Buildings that have been bombed always look better after a few days, even though only the glass is swept up and the windows are covered with boarding. Dirt settling on the structures seems to dress their wounds. On the other hand, streets that have been bombed always look worse after a week or so because the repair squads invariably have to enlarge the crater three or four times its original size before they can complete the necessary repairs. Among items no one has bothered to repair or replace are clocks on public buildings. Most of those not smashed to smithereens have broken faces and drooping hands. Sandbags and white curb markings, which were the distinguishing features of London's face in the early months of the war, have now almost completely disappeared.

LONDON STANDS UP TO THE BLITZKRIEG

Even the sandbags around Eros's statue in Piccadilly Circus were removed recently after rot had set in.

Although most night attacks on London through November and December were only slightly more severe than the nuisance raids of last summer, no one thought that the lull would continue for long, so the blitz life went on much the same as in September and October. Londoners, accustomed to and toughened by intense raids, feel a certain sense of relief when the sirens howl and the banging and whistling of bombs and gunfire begins. On nights when there is scarcely any anti-aircraft barrage, many people complain that they can't sleep because it's too quiet. On such nights, however, they can repeatedly hear the one sound which terrifies them, though in ninety-nine cases out of a hundred their fears are unwarranted. It is the long, whistling swish that a bomb makes hurtling through the air. The reason Londoners hear this sound so often is that it is often undistinguishable from the noise made by the tires and motor of a fast-approaching automobile. During the day, if there's a raid on, it's not at all unusual for office workers and housewives to dive under desks or tables when a car goes by outside, as nervous Americans duck when a truck backfires.

On the whole, however, Londoners refuse to be concerned about daylight air attacks unless gunfire and bomb explosions can actually be heard. When they wish to know whether a raid is in progress or not, they look for the nearest bobby, who during raids is required to move his gas mask from hip to chest, where it's more accessible. Incidentally, the bobbies discarded their famous high-domed navy-blue hats when the blitz started. They now wear steel helmets at all times.

One effect of the blitz has been to create a rush for apartments in tall, reinforced-concrete buildings. Even blocks of flats that have been hit, such as big Dolphin Court along the Thames, are turning hundreds away daily. On the other hand, magnificent old houses and apartments in once fashionable but now deserted squares like Belgrave and Kensington can be had almost for nothing on a month-to-month basis. About the only accommodations now available in steel buildings are on the top two floors. These are in small demand because Rule No. 1 for safety in air raids is to be under at least three floors of concrete. Most people prefer the second or third floors of a seven- (or more) story building. There they are comparatively safe from any bombs landing in the street and from a direct hit on top of the building. The risk of one crashing in at an angle is not much greater than the risk of being trapped in a shelter.

More than a million Londoners still spend the nights in public shelters. Some do so out of habit, some for safety's sake, some because they have no homes, and some because they want to make sure, by regular attendance, of keeping their places.

The other 5,000,000 people still left in London either sleep in Anderson shelters or in their homes. Of the latter, about two-thirds stay in their bedrooms.

The 200 largest shelters, holding a total of 100,000 people, are now nearly all equipped with first-aid posts, with a nurse attached to each all night and a doctor paying at least one visit an evening. Bunks have been provided for 270,000 shelterites, and it's only a question of time before enough will be available for everyone. The 150,000 who sleep in the tube stations can buy sixpenny snacks of tea, cake, and chocolate at various times in the evening. The food arrives in "Refreshments Special" trains, and is served by 1,000 girls in green overalls and red turbans who make $7 a week. Nearly all the other shelters in London either have canteens on the premises or are served nightly by mobile canteens belonging to the Borough Councils.

Life in the shelters has been considerably more satisfactory than was anticipated. On the whole, the people are in exceptionally good health and humor, and the only thing they really miss is family privacy. Members of all classes are beginning to know, like, and understand one another. In the evenings office boys play cards or darts with their bosses, and in the morning charwomen awaken Civil Servants by tweaking their toes. At dances, which most shelters now hold weekly, waiters waltz with the ladies they served earlier in the day, and managing directors fox-trot with the barmaids who sold them their morning glasses of ale.

About once a week every big shelter is invaded by a Government-sponsored group of entertainers. Recently actor-comedian George Formby, the idol of the working classes, sang and played his ukulele to the thousands who shelter in the Aldwych tube station. His master of ceremonies was none other than the officer commanding the London shelters, Sir Edward ("Evans of the Broke") Evans. Newspapers are also working overtime to keep the shelter world from getting bored. Columns entitled "Here Are Some Shelter Games" now occupy regular places in the newspapers, along with crossword puzzles and cartoons. A typical suggestion is to pick a "world's all-time champion cricket eleven" or a team whose members' names all begin with "H."

Outside of the damage done by bombs and their effect on the city's sleeping habits, the state of siege in which London lives is revealed less by any dramatic change in its weathered and grimy exterior than by small and unpredictable details. For instance, since the public can no longer buy automobiles, London streets are now filled with noisy, sputtering jalopies which in the United States could only be seen in secondhand-car lots or junk yards. There are more flying about now than at any time since the war started, because the Government recently introduced a "free lift" scheme whereby motorists who offer rides to people normally using trains or busses get an extra allowance of petrol. The thoroughfares are also crowded with double-decker busses of almost every color in the spectrum. The cardinal of London Transport of course predominates, but there are also the maroon busses of Leeds, the red of Manchester, the blue and cream of Edinburgh, and scores of others which were rushed to London to bolster the overtaxed transportation systems when the blitz reached its autumn peak. On some busses gray-and-blue uniformed girls have replaced men as bus conductors. Among them are a number of attractive chorus girls, who still wear silk stockings, high-heeled shoes, and plenty of lipstick.

Downtown London is still much more an area of busy shops and throbbing thoroughfares than of ugly ruins and gaping craters. Striking, however, are the tiny shop windows in acreages of beaverboard or wood sometimes extending the length of a city block. The shopkeepers went in for wood and composition frontings because glass is hard to get and too expensive to replace every few days when a bomb falls in the neighborhood. At first they painted advertisements on the exteriors, such as "Be bombed in comfort—buy one of our camp beds," but lately the trend has been toward fancy colored illustrations of the products for sale inside. Curiously, the smaller windows draw bigger crowds than do the normal-sized ones.

One of the few touches of make-up on the gray, drab face of the center of town is provided by the great signs and posters on buildings and billboards boosting the nation's war effort. Herbert Morrison's slogan "Go to It" flashes across at least one building in every block. In Piccadilly Circus alone there are reminders to "Dig for Victory," to "Save Your Way to Victory, Buy National Certificates," and that "The Fighting Forces Need Your Binoculars, Take Them to Your Nearest Optician." Other signs that add color are the notices hung on certain bombed stores threatening "Looters" with prosecution and the "Business As Usual" slogans on the exteriors of almost every bombed shop still functioning. Fox-caped prostitutes plying their trade (mostly in the afternoons now, rather than the evenings) in front of the latter notices cause Londoners to smile.

Stores are still bursting with goods, but this will only be true for a short time, because the Government recently issued an order limiting retailers' further purchases, particularly of wooden, leather, and metal goods, to about one-third of the pre-blitz average. In recent weeks shortages of certain things have already been noticeable. Tailors, for example, with urgent orders for uniforms found that they had used up their month's quota of pins, and had to put little boy and girl apprentices to work searching for them between the floor boards. The shortage of hairpins is so acute that many women, especially those in the services, are having their hair bobbed. Soon it will be almost impossible to purchase such things as nail files, tweezers, and manicure scissors, while some chemist shops already limit the sale of soap to one bar at a time to each customer. There is nothing, of course, to prevent a person from returning a few minutes later for a second purchase. When the Government imposed a ban on the sale of silk stockings, women rushed to stores to lay in supplies, which they are saving for night and Sunday wear. Meanwhile, lisle and heavy black woolen hose have become daytime fashion for the winter. Because women can spend only six cents per week on cosmetics, women's-page editors are advising their readers to rub lipstick in well so as not to lose it on cigarette ends and glasses, and not automatically to dab powder on their faces every time they peer into their compacts. "Cosmetics," the newspapers warn, "are now a luxury—not an absent-minded indulgence."

As the amount and type of goods shopkeepers can sell become more limited and the public's purchasing power dwindles, the people on the streets are looking shabbier and shabbier. London women have never been stylish, but this winter, in their two- and three-year-old coats and hats, they look especially down at heel. Men wear old tan raincoats and suits which go unpressed from one month to the next. The faces of the people are haggard as a result of sleepless nights, worries, and long hours of duty in the civilian services. Londoners bearing any signs of injuries from air raids, however, are as rare as Indians on the streets of New York. No one is able to explain the reason why. Another phenomenon is the complete absence of funeral processions despite the heavy death tolls of the past four months.

The food situation is slowly getting worse, but not in a quantitative sense, for Londoners are still eating as much as ever. Present stocks are sufficient to feed the whole nation for a year, even if imports were cut off entirely. There are not, however, nearly so many kinds of food available as in pre-blitz days, and the quality is beginning to decline. Onions, lemons, baking chocolate, and bananas are almost nonexistent, and before long the remaining stocks of canned goods will be used up. Fancy cookies are stocked only by the higher-priced shops, like Fortnum & Mason and Selfridge's provisions store. The ration of beef, pork, lamb, and bacon isn't large enough to satisfy the average appetite, but this gap in the diet is easily filled with such unrationed items as fowl, liver, tongue, brains, etc. The only foods which the average Londoners would like to have in larger quantities are butter, sugar, and perhaps tea —but the Londoner drinks more tea than is good for him anyway. Certain foods, when they are obtainable, are also getting too expensive for the lower and middle classes. Grapefruit, for example, cost twenty-five cents apiece, while eggs fetch eighty-two cents a dozen.

Restaurants, except for having to comply with the Government's order forbidding them to serve both meat and fish courses to one customer, haven't been feeling the pinch very much until recently, when their supplies of rationed meats were cut to one-fourth the normal supply. Sugar and butter are served in scanty portions. Even at the best hotels, like the Ritz and the Dorchester, guests get only one tiny lump of sugar for each cup of beverage and a piece of butter no bigger than a fingernail for a whole meal. A bigger problem to restaurant owners than food supplies, however, is keeping their businesses going with practically no night trade. Their only solution is to drum up enough lunch customers to pack the restaurant for three or four sittings. Many have been able to do this quite successfully, because the majority of Londoners now entertain at lunch instead of at dinner and because some of the best foreign restaurants closed down when the owners were interned.

Having caught their breath again when the Luftwaffe laid off the capital for a few weeks, London soon began looking for entertainment in the afternoons and evenings. Myra Hess's noontime musicales in the basement of the National Gallery have been such a success that she plans to continue them till the end of the war. Likewise Producer Herbert Farjeon started rehearsals just before Christmas on a new review to replace *Diversion* (named after the ubiquitous yellow police notices detouring traffic around unexploded bombs), which is playing to full houses in a Charing Cross Road theater every afternoon. The Café de Paris, for years one of the gayest night spots in town, is now open at noon and puts on a floor show during lunch. In the late afternoon, officers on leave take their ladies to the Piccadilly Hotel for tea dancing or to a Lyons Corner House, where eight-piece bands play such tunes as *Rose of Tralee* and *Begin the Beguine* while the customers consume their sixpennyworth of tea and crumpets.

When blackout time approaches around 5:15 P.M. the underground cocktail bars at places like the Ritz or Merrie's Club in Baker Street begin to fill up. Those who go for the first time invariably glance at the ceiling on entering to satisfy themselves that it is solidly built. Londoners also do their dining and dancing underground, or at least under five or six floors of concrete building. At the Lansdowne House restaurant, where Prince von Starhemberg escorts his lovelies almost nightly, guests sit at a fifteen- or twenty-degree angle facing the orchestra. The room, designed as a movie theater, was converted into a restaurant when the Government decided it wanted the regular restaurant for a shelter for the Ministry of Shipping. With the price of a dinner at the elegant Hungaria Restaurant off Piccadilly Circus goes the privilege of sleeping in a cot on the premises or the right to a free ride home in a taxicab.

There are only two shows functioning at night in London and they are the same two that hung on during the worst period of the blitz. One is at the Windmill Theater, which puts on a kind of glorified burlesque, called *Revudeville,* for an audience composed mostly of bald-headed businessmen from the provinces. The other is the Players' Club, which temporarily moved to Author Anthony Berkeley's house in St. John's Wood when bombs fell uncomfortably near its Covent Garden quarters and has now settled down in the underground premises of a defunct night club near the Ritz Hotel. While the audience eats hot dogs and drinks beer, the players entertain with Victorian songs and skits. Among the performers is beauteous young Joanna Horder, niece of the King's physician, Lord Horder, who is making a big hit with a teasing number called *You Are a Very Very Very Handsome Man.* Six nights a week, the club is jammed with some of the most prominent people in London, including Ministry of Information and Foreign Office bigwigs, theatrical folk, artists, publishers, etc., who dance and have snacks with the cast after the show. Around midnight the party breaks up, but if the night is noisy, the majority curl up on the chairs and sofas till morning.

A few days before Christmas, Mayfair socialites, the diplomatic set, and a large number of men and women in the fighting services forgot the war for one night and attended a Blitz Ball (for charity) at Grosvenor House. It was the first time since the summer that a big crowd had assembled in formal clothes. Judging from the gaiety of the party, no one would have imagined that a battle was raging in the skies that very evening. Luckily, the big guns in Hyde Park across the street were muffled by the booming orchestra. The only reminder of the war was a delightful ditty sung by Magda Kun, a pretty Hungarian entertainer. The chorus goes:

> I've got a cozy flat,
> There's a place for your hat,
> I'll wear a pink chiffon negligee gown;
> And do I know my stuff,
> But if that's not enough
> I've got the deepest shelter in town.

Londoners are still going to the movies (open only in the afternoons), but not so much to get vicarious thrills from the daredevil exploits and romantic love-makings of Hollywood stars as to take their minds off the war. Britons now have their own heroes and heroines in the persons of the men in the R.A.F. and A.R.P. and the women in the W.R.N.S., W.A.F.S., and A.T.S. On this subject, the *Daily Herald's* ace columnist Hannen Swaffer recently wrote: "We look nowadays with cynicism at the names of much-boosted film stars whose screened exhibits used to thrill. Clark Gable— who is he anyway? Nearby any cinema which boosts his prowess A.R.P. workers sleep by hundreds—unknown men and women who when darkness falls will risk danger of which he never dreamed." Several of London's biggest motion-picture houses had their faces badly smashed by a land mine which fell in Leicester Square, but at others record crowds have been queueing to see Bette Davis and Charles Boyer in *All This and Heaven Too* and Charlie Chaplin in *The Great Dictator*. A number of pictures are also being made in London studios, including Shaw's *Major Barbara,* with Wendy Hiller of *Pygmalion* fame; *Kipps,* with Michael Redgrave and Dianna Wynyard; and an *Empire Is Built,* starring John Gielgud.

But for the great majority of Londoners, who haven't the money, inclination, or the opportunity to look for things to do in the West End, life under the blitz has become very standardized and, except for the bombings, very dull. The days of Sunday excursions to the sea or South Downs have been over for months. (The only out-of-town trips Londoners now take are visits to the 2,000,000 women and children evacuees.) If the menfolk aren't working in the factories or offices on Sunday, they probably spend the day digging in the garden or helping their friends repair bomb damage. Aside from their journeys to and from work, the men rarely leave their own neighborhood, either because traveling is too difficult and dangerous at night or because they are occupied with civilian-service duties. For the same reasons, women stay near home both day and night; indeed, tens of thousands of them haven't even been to central London since the blitz.

Government influence on the newspapers, the curtailment of radio programs, the lack of effective opposition in Parliament, the common hardships, dangers, and form of living have also tended to make people think alike and adopt similar tastes, mannerisms, expressions, etc. For instance, there is a general agreement that personal experiences with a bomb are taboo as a topic of conversation. This is because no one in London is interested in any bombing story but his own. When people gather they also make a point of neither commenting on air-raid warnings nor letting them cause the slightest interruption in the conversation.

The enforced trend toward uniformity has led thousands of Londoners to read such books as *Guilty Men* and *War by Revolution,* both vicious indictments of the past leaders in Britain; to play chess; to consume large quantities of Bovril, which is cleverly advertised by drawings of bomb-disposal men strolling nonchalantly away from a giant bomb and one of them saying, "I think we've just got time for a hot Bovril,

224

old man"; to refer to the present period as "the blitz"; to make such comments as "quiet night" or "a bit noisy tonight" instead of the usual clichés about the weather; to sleep with their wallets and purses under their pillows; to acclaim radio broadcasters like J. B. Priestley and entertainers like Churchill's son-in-law, Vic Oliver; to hum such tunes as *I've Got My Eyes on You* and *I'm Nobody's Baby;* to glance automatically at the sky when they step out into the open at night; and to do a hundred and one other things that everybody else is doing.

Londoners all agree that the King and Queen are carrying on nobly in their positions as symbolic commanders of the male and female fighting and civilian forces. Although they may consider Winston Churchill something of a clown at times, they believe that he is *the* man to beat Hitler. Because of Winston's genius, Londoners are willing to overlook the fact that he's a member, indeed the leader, of the Conservative Party, which they've detested ever since they woke up to the failures of the Chamberlain government. A story about Winston Churchill that is currently making the luncheon-table rounds concerns a Cabinet meeting during which a Minister asked Churchill why he didn't order the R.A.F. to give the Nazis a few doses of their own medicine by bombing the civilian sections of large German cities. The Prime Minister replied, "Gentlemen, such action would indeed be a delectable pleasure, but I want you to know that I am a man of principle. So for me business must come before pleasure."

The Germans are said to be greatly puzzled over London's willingness to take continuous punishment without so much as a thought of surrender. The British, they think, are licked and refuse to accept the fact. But the British are not by any means licked, and if, in the end, they win the war, it will be owing in no small measure to the magnificent way in which the people of London are standing up to the siege.